D0416832

COMPASSION IS THE BUGLER

COMPASSION IS THE BUGLER

The Struggle for Animal Rights

by

Clive Hollands

Foreword by Rt. Hon. Lord Houghton of Sowerby C.H.

MACDONALD PUBLISHERS
EDINBURGH

ISBN 0 904265 35 8

Published by
Macdonald Publishers Edinburgh
Edgefield Road, Loanhead, Midlothian.

Printed by
Macdonald Printers (Edinburgh) Limited
Edgefield Road, Loanhead, Midlothian

TO

Fay—my wife, whose encouragement and forbearance with my nomadic way of life, makes my work and this book possible.

Acknowledgements

I should like to express my thanks to Lord Houghton for his advice and suggestions on the manuscript; to my assistant, Les Ward, for reading the manuscript; to my secretary Marie Flockhart, for typing; to Jaime Lass for indexing; to Sean Chapman for my title; and finally, to the many animal welfare societies and the thousands of individuals who supported Animal Welfare Year and the campaign to "Put Animals Into Politics"—and who by so doing were responsible for the publication of this book. A particular debt of gratitude is also owed to my former assistants, David Martin and Gennie Poole; my cashier, Mrs Doris Taylor; Rosemary Reilly; Margaret Ramsay; and Pat Chapman of Infopress Ltd.

List of Abbreviations

AA	Animal Advocates Information Service Ltd
AWT	Animal Welfare Trust
AWY	Animal Welfare Year
BFSS	British Field Sports Society
BHS	British Horse Society
BUAV	British Union for the Abolition of Vivisection
BVA	British Veterinary Association
BWC	Beauty Without Cruelty
CCC	Christian Consultative Council for the Welfare of Animals
CIWF	Compassion in World Farming
CPL	Cats Protection League
CRAE	Committee for the Reform of Animal Experimentation
CSCAW	Catholic Study Circle for Animal Welfare
FAWC	Farm Animal Welfare Council
FAWCE	Farm Animal Welfare Co-ordinating Executive
FRAME	Fund for the Replacement of Animals in Medical Experiments
GECCAP	General Election Co-ordinating Committee for Animal Protection
HEC	Humane Education Council
HSA	Hunt Saboteurs Association
IFAW	International Fund for Animal Welfare
ISPA	International Society for the Protection of Animals

JACOPIS	Joint Advisory Committee on Pets in Society
LACS	League Against Cruel Sports
NAVS	National Anti-Vivisection Society
NCCAP	National Consultative Committee for Animal Protection
NCDL	National Canine Defence League
NFU	National Farmers' Union
NJEWC	National Joint Equine Welfare Committee
PDSA	Peoples' Dispensary for Sick Animals
POLG	Protect Our Livestock Group
RCVS	Royal College of Veterinary Surgeons
RSPB	Royal Society for the Protection of Birds
RSPCA	Royal Society for the Prevention of Cruelty to Animals
St AAF	St. Andrew Animal Fund
SAVS	Scottish Anti-Vivisection Society
SPANA	Society for the Protection of Animals in North Africa
SPCA	Society for the Prevention of Cruelty to Animals
SSPV	Scottish Society for the Prevention of Vivisection
SUPA	Society of United Prayer for Animals
UFAW	Universities Federation for Animal Welfare
WFPA	World Federation for the Protection of Animals
WWF	World Wildlife Fund

CONTENTS

FOREWORD by the Rt. Hon. Lord Houghton of Sowerby C.H.

PREFACE

INTRODUCTION

PART 1—ANIMALS, THE SOCIETIES AND THE LAW

Chapter   I   -   What We Do to Animals

            II   -   The Animal Societies—"Where Did They All Come From?"

            III   -   Charity Law and the Animal Welfare Societies

            IV   -   The Law and Animals

PART 2—ANIMAL WELFARE YEAR

            V   -   The Early Struggle

            VI   -   "And Some Fell on Stony Ground"

            VII   -   The Run-up to the Year and Near Disaster

            VIII   -   National and Major Local Events of the Year

            IX   -   Publicity

            X   -   Areas of Concern and the Joint Consultative Bodies

            XI   -   "Not an End in Itself—But Rather a Beginning"

PART 3—"PUTTING ANIMALS INTO POLITICS"

XII - General Election Co-ordinating Committee for Animal Protection

XIII - The Party Conferences

XIV - Continuing Action and Political Debate

XV - The Importance of Publicity from the "Opposition"

XVI - The General Election

PART 4—THE FUTURE FOR ANIMALS AND ANIMAL WELFARE

XVII - Are We Making Any Progress?

XVIII - Public and Private Attitudes

XIX - Compassion is the Bugler

APPENDICES

NOTES

INDEX

FOREWORD

RT. HON. LORD HOUGHTON OF SOWERBY CH

Had the author written an allegorical tale he would have told of the animals' crusade to Westminster where, it was said, humans "made noises just like animals". Actually the humans at Westminster made noises just like humans. For centuries they had assembled there for the purpose of asserting their sovereign authority. They opened their proceedings with daily prayer for blessings and guidance, followed by heated debate on the selfish aims of men.

Long before history began, and long afterwards, no cruelty was too hideous and no torture too unspeakable to stand in the way of the attainment of man's dominion. Human rights excluded all others; human needs subordinated all others; human greed sacrificed all others: humans took all.

This is the setting to the movement for the rights of non-human species. It is one of a deeply entrenched belief that the living world was put there for the express use, benefit and enjoyment of mankind. The more "civilised" man has become the greater the menace to the animal kingdom. The natural world of thousands of millions of years is now threatened by the infestation of this planet and the exploitations of all its resources by human beings.

Now, at last, and hopefully not too late, a feeling of concern, even of apprehension, about the devastating consequences of the rake's progress of mankind is spreading throughout the world. An enlightened change in values accepts that human rights, though still paramount, are by no means exclusive of the right of other species. We are now much more rational and scientific about the origin of man and his place in the history of life on earth. We now see the world in the round. We no longer base our attitude towards the animal kingdom upon the presumptions of a divine purpose in the creation of man which cast all other living things (including some ethnic groups of humans) into a condition of subordination and enslavement ordained by God.

This world-wide trend towards better understanding of the infinite variety and priceless value of our heritage from the timeless

xiii

past has still to develop the force of political influence and power. While the eventual solutions to this, as to many other issues, calls for a global strategy, the base camp is the nation state. The strength of international action is then the combined strength of all.

This book contains the story of recent efforts in this country to convert widely held public opinion into political action. The point is reached in public affairs when a response by governments is needed to stir the wind of change. That point is reached when public sentiment and public concern becomes a demand for action. While public attitudes can achieve much, action on many aspects of the conservation of species and the protection of animals from evil requires the force of law.

That requires action by governments. In many countries action by governments is brought about by political and parliamentary pressures. The United Kingdom is one of those countries and that is why it became necessary to put animals into politics at a time when policies and programmes were being prepared.

And so, when a general election in Britain could be anticipated in late 1978, the first attempt was made to mobilise public opinion for the single purpose of persuading the political parties contesting seats in parliament to declare their intentions about the protection of animals.

The author, Clive Hollands, is uniquely qualified to write the history of this important and fruitful campaign. He was the secretary to the task force of this movement into the jungle of politics, from which we emerged into the light to see much of our purpose written into the manifestos of the principal political parties. The two main areas of promised attention—treatment of farm animals, and scientific use of living animals—are of international importance. Satisfactory changes in both areas are unlikely without inter-nation co-operation. Although the full effectiveness of national action is limited, this obviously could lead to community action in the EEC and the Council of Europe.

Clive Hollands has told something of the difficulties of getting "animal lobbies" to work together, even when common effort is clearly called for. There are numerous reasons for this; not all of them comprehensible. The restraints put upon voluntary societies by our Charity Acts are certainly inhibiting when campaigning for changes in the law. But rivalries come into it as well. Unlike political parties, trade unions and professional bodies, charitable bodies appear to lack the degree of self-interest indispensable to successful collective action. Charities tend to be divided by common purposes and have many understandable worries about their continued dependence upon voluntary support.

Perhaps in our impatience for action and the plain necessity of getting political parties committed on measures for animal welfare during the run up to the election in 1979, we regarded the difficulties too lightly. Notwithstanding many strains on the way we did succeed in putting animals into British politics for the first time ever. And in politics the animals will stay. Progress will be all the quicker and all the better for that.

What this book shows is while charities do good, they cannot fight political battles.

Only those societies which have foregone the benefit of tax and rating exemptions are completely free to join the pressure groups in our politics. It was they who made possible this story of how we thrust the cause of animals into an arena erstwhile fully occupied by humans making noises like humans.

PREFACE

To most of us there comes a moment in life, usually well after the first flush of youth, when we ask ourselves the question, "What am I doing with my life?" The majority then turn over and go to sleep and although the question may surface again in the mind from time to time, that is the end of the matter.

My own moment of truth came when I had reached the age of thirty years or so and I suddenly knew there must be more to life than making money for other people. Until that time, after serving seven years in the Royal Navy, I had been quite content working in the London office of an American oil tanker company, where I was employed as Deputy Marine Personnel Superintendent, a post with very good prospects.

Some five years and hundreds of applications later, and owing largely to the encouragement I received from my wife not to throw in the sponge, I obtained the job I wanted, that of Assistant Secretary of the Scottish Society for the Prevention of Vivisection, based in Edinburgh. At last I was working in animal welfare.

Seen from the outside, the job of an animal welfare society is simple. Britain is an "animal loving" country where cruelty would not be tolerated, and therefore the societies merely have to draw cases of cruelty to the attention of the authorities. The offenders are then dealt with in the courts.

Once I was on the "inside" of the movement, however, I quickly realised my error. My first impression was one of complete bewilderment. The multiplicity of animal welfare societies worried me and the knowledge that people were capable of doing the things they did to animals and that the law permitted them to do it shocked me, just as did the fact that the rest of us, knowing what they did, allowed them to continue doing it.

In my spare time I studied the history of the animal welfare movement and the legislation which governed the ways in which animals may be exploited for the benefit of man. Since nearly all legislation results from pressure on government to act, it was quite clear from the very weaknesses of animal welfare and protective legislation that the animal lobby was not achieving its purpose. At that time, since I was a "new boy", there was little I could do to bring about a change. In 1970, however, after I succeeded Harvey Metcalfe as Director of the Scottish Society and Secretary of the St Andrew Animal Fund, my opportunity came at a conference of Scottish animal welfare societies organised by the Fund in 1973.

One of the Fund's directors, Mr Christopher Mylne, the naturalist and film-maker, drew attention to the fact that 1976 would mark the centenary of the *Cruelty to Animals Act, 1876,* and suggested marking the event by holding an Animal Welfare Year. This proposal was taken up by the guest speaker Mr F. A. Burden, M.P., and so the idea was born and my chance had come.

This book is largely the history of two campaigns—Animal Welfare Year (1976/1977) and the campaign which followed to "Put Animals Into Politics" (1978/1979). It is a story of success—and of failure—but it is also one of hope. It is my hope that all who read it, whether "inside" or "outside" the movement, will gain encouragement and the determination to continue the struggle.

Edinburgh.   C.H.

INTRODUCTION

I lost count of the number of well-intentioned people, many with a lifetime of experience in animal welfare, who told me, "It's impossible—it won't work," or "You mean well Clive, but it's all been tried before." They assured me that the animal welfare organisations just would not work together.

Admittedly the two examples of co-operative action which I had witnessed during the short time I had been in the movement, the British Council of Anti-Vivisection Societies and the ill-fated Association of British Anti-Vivisection Societies, had both "died the death." Nevertheless, I knew there had to be a way. The fact that attempts to bring unity had failed in the past was no reason for giving up—*if it was the right way and the only way to make progress.*

I was determined from the outset that Animal Welfare Year was going to succeed in spite of all obstacles and difficulties, many of which occurred in the two-and-a-half years it took to organise the Year. Before I come to the history of the campaigns, however, I have devoted the opening chapters of this book to a brief account of the animal welfare movement in this country and of the legislation which relates to the protection and welfare of animals.

First of all, it is important to know what we are talking about. What do we mean by animal welfare? This is what, in my opinion, it is not.

It is not conservation. Conservation, which may be important in its own right, is the protection of endangered species by taking such steps as banning the killing of the species or protecting its habitat. Perhaps the most endangered species on this planet at the present time are the whales. This great family of animals, which includes the blue whale, the largest animal which has ever inhabited the earth, is endangered because man has relentlessly hunted and slaughtered it for its oils, blubber and meat.

The whale is probably the most intelligent animal in the world, other than man, (if you need convincing you only need to listen to the record of the song of the humpback whale), yet we still allow man to hunt this magnificent creature and subject it to a slow and agonising death. The International Whaling Commission and the governments of the world make attempts to control whaling in order to preserve the species. Note that they aim only to preserve and conserve the species, not to ban for ever the monstrous obscenity of such slaughter.

Neither is animal welfare being an "animal-lover." In Great Britain there are estimated to be over twenty million household pets including over five million dogs, three million cats and five million birds, all owned by people the majority of whom would refer to themselves as "animal lovers."[1] How many of these millions of pet-owners are concerned however over the plight of the laboratory rat or the battery chicken? Not many. In fact it is true to say that a proportion of them do not even "love" their own pets. A great deal of suffering is inflicted on pets, not usually as a result of deliberate cruelty, although such cases still happen far too frequently, but as a result of ignorance and indifference. A dog is a dog, not a toy for a child or a status symbol for an adult. It needs food (and not too much) and regular exercise. Without doubt the worst suffering is caused by over-breeding which results in enormous numbers of unwanted dogs and cats, the majority of which become strays and return to a semi-wild state or are rounded up for the state or the animal welfare societies to kill.

Nor is it "kindness to animals," a phrase which can mean anything or, more often, nothing. How frequently have I heard those directly involved in the worst forms of animal exploitation protest, "But we are *kind* to our animals."

What then is animal welfare? An article in the *Veterinary Record* a few years ago commented:

> The intention is to note the continued advance on several fronts, towards reducing the status and *natural dignity of animals,* regarding them as chattels; seeing little or nothing objectionable in their increasing exploitation; arriving finally—by such gradual process of thought and custom as to be apparent only to the discerning—at a state of mind when liberty to eat and breathe are the only liberties animals have left.[2]

This then would be my definition of animal welfare: dignity—according to animals the natural dignity which is due to them as living, sentient creatures.

To my mind, animal welfare has nothing to do with whether or not animals live or die, even if this means extinction. When the last great whale dies, as it probably will, it will not be the whale's loss, for never again will man be able to inflict that terrible mutilation upon its body. It is man's loss, for he will have destroyed for ever the largest animal to have lived on earth.

My only concern is the suffering we inflict on animals, whether it be for food, clothing, knowledge, sport or pleasure. If we could learn to respect and accord to animals the dignity which is their due as living beings, suffering, pain and torment would end.

Part One

ANIMALS, THE SOCIETIES AND THE LAW

WHAT WE DO TO ANIMALS

Some 200 years ago Jeremy Bentham stated in his *Introduction to the Principles of Morals and Legislation:*

> The day may come when the rest of the animal creation may acquire those rights which never could have been withholden from them, but by the hand of tyranny.

Animals have inhabited this earth for a very long time. When man, the newcomer, was "given dominion" over all other creatures, his tyranny began and animals have suffered relentlessly at his hands right up to the present day. Yet throughout history, in spite of his cruelty to the other species, man has made animals his closest companions and on occasion has worshipped them as deities.

Many of the barbarities of the past have now vanished and modern man may look back in horror at the cruelties inflicted on animals during the "dark ages." But is the treatment we mete out to animals today to provide food, clothing, sport, pleasure and knowledge really any better? Are we more civilised in our attitude to other species?

Farming for food

Animals and birds have been intensively farmed since the time when man first had the idea of putting a fence round a field to keep his beasts in one place. Over the centuries, farm animals have been bred and cross-bred to produce more meat and less fat, more breast and less leg, more milk, more eggs, and so on until they have come to be the domesticated creatures we know today. They may be creatures much removed in appearance from their wild forebears, but they still possess many of the same behavioural needs.

The majority of farmers show concern for their stock and spend long hours caring for them, but modern intensive farming is another matter altogether. Intensive farming, or as it is more commonly known, factory farming, has turned living animals into food-producing machines on a factory assembly line principle. In

3

such systems the animals' needs are sacrificed to achieve maximum output of flesh, eggs or milk for the minimum input of labour, feed, heating and lighting.

The condition of the intensively farmed animal and the growth of such production line methods in Britain was first highlighted in Ruth Harrison's book, *Animal Machines*[1], and the resulting storm of public protest led to the Government setting up a committee of enquiry under the chairmanship of the late Professor Rogers Brambell. The report of this committee, known as the Brambell Report[2], made a number of recommendations for the protection of animals reared in intensive systems. The most important of these recommendations became known as "the five freedoms":

> An animal should at least have sufficient freedom of movement to be able without difficulty to turn round, groom itself, get up, lie down and stretch its limbs.

It was not much; but it was something. But even that modicum of protection was too much for the Government, and when it eventually acted on the Brambell Report, only some of the recommendations were accepted, these being incorporated into codes of practice which were not mandatory.

It is not my opinion that depriving animals of green fields and the wind on their faces is necessarily cruel. It is when animals are deprived of the opportunity to indulge in their natural behavioural patterns that suffering and stress result. To quote one example: the chicken is reputed to have a very simple brain, but nevertheless has three basic drives:

1. to establish its position within the "pecking order" of the flock;
2. to peck and scratch for its food; and
3. to indulge in nesting behaviour.

In the modern battery system of egg production, where hens are kept three, four or sometimes even more to a cage measuring fifteen inches by nineteen inches standing on wire mesh floors so that their eggs and excreta can drop through, they are deprived of the opportunity to indulge in any of their natural behavioural patterns for the whole of their miserable laying life of a year or so before they are slaughtered to make chicken soup.

Other intensive systems are as bad: veal calves living their

4

. . . and this book is about creatures great and small. *(Photograph by courtesy of "Express & Star", Wolverhampton).*

Animals are in the news.

"World Day of Prayer for Animals".
Blessing of Pets Service, Shere Parish Church, 4th October 1979.
(Photograph by courtesy of "Surrey Advertiser".)

"Tara"—part Scottish wildcat.

The Author's Animals (some of them) *(Photographs by courtesy of John Thomson)*

"Toby, Sally and Twizzy"

Lord Houghton of Sowerby with the author at the dinner given in 1979 to honour Lord Houghton.

thirteen week lives in solid-sided crates with slatted floors and no bedding, are fed on a milk substitute diet with none of the roughage, for which they crave, all in order to keep the flesh white. Pigs are raised in sweat-boxes to increase the rate of growth, while the condition of the breeding sows that produce them is often unspeakable.

The recent BBC television programme *Down on the Factory Farm,* screened in 1979, could have left viewers in no doubt as to the abject misery of animals reared under these conditions. It is said that food prices would at least double if intensive systems of rearing were banned, but this programme demonstrated that such claims are totally untrue. Viewers were taken to a pig-farm, a veal calf producer and a "strawyard" for egg production where farmers, who had adapted extensive traditional methods to suit present day economic restrictions, were competing with intensive producers and still making a fair profit.

I believe that even if this were not so, we must be prepared to pay a higher price for our food. Up until a few years ago the western world enjoyed cheap oil, sugar, coffee, tea and many other products which were cheap because they were produced on the suffering and the poverty of the people living largely in the Third World. That situation has now dramatically changed and we have to pay the full economic price for the materials and food they produce. The time must come—and I can only hope that its coming will not be too long delayed—when mankind must accept that we cannot enjoy cheap food obtained at the price of the suffering and the agony of the animal kingdom.

Clothing

Men, and more particularly women, have worn the furs of animals to clothe themselves in past centuries as a matter of necessity. In more modern times this has been done merely as a symbol of status and affluence.

Although some fur-bearing animals, notably mink, chinchilla and sometimes foxes are reared in captivity by intensive farming methods, euphemistically referred to as "ranching," the majority of pelts still come from wild animals trapped in the snare or the vicious leg-hold trap. The agony of an animal caught by the leg (imagine your hand trapped in the door of a car), can be measured not in hours, but often in days. Now multiply the suffering of one such animal by between sixty and one hundred times, the number of pelts required for a full-length coat, and you now have the real cost of that luxurious fur, the price in money and the higher price in a mountain of suffering.

Before leaving trapping, I must make a final point: the trap cannot distinguish between the animal with the valuable fur and one that has no commercial value. It has been estimated that for every valuable pelt, the trappers discard two or three of what they call "trash," animals or birds with no value. For this reason the toll in animal life is many more times the number of pelts sold each year in the worlds fur auctions.

The annual massacre of the "whitecoat," the baby of the harp seal in the Gulf of St. Lawrence, has aroused the anger of the world, but the Canadian Government will not bring to an end this blot on the name of Canada. The quota set each year for the kill in March is in the region of one hundred and eighty thousand "whitecoats," all of which will be clubbed to death so that women in Europe may wear sealskin.

In Britain in 1978 the Secretary of State for Scotland was forced by public opinion to abandon the larger part of the cull of the grey seal in the Orkneys, where it was proposed that nine hundred females and four thousand pups were to be slaughtered because of "damage to fish stocks." If a cull were necessary, and the Government's scientific evidence was far from proving such necessity, it would have made sense to cull adult seals. The late Sir Frank Fraser Darling, an acknowledged expert on the grey seal commented:

> I favour some cull of adults when they come ashore in early September. There is then a chance to do the horrible job quietly and leave October quiet for the main calving season.[3]

But there is no commercial value in the scarred pelt of an adult seal; it is the soft and unmarked skin on the newly born pup that fur dealers want. In his book *Between Animal and Man* Dr Michael Fox discusses the fur trade and comments on the luxury furs:

> They are contaminated, unclean and unworthy adornments for our sisters of the earth. They are for the dead in mind and spirit, who display their ignorance adorned in the vain luxury of wild fur—wild fur which, in its richness and softness, stifles the scream of man's inhumanity to his fellow creatures.[4]

Sport and pleasure

It was once remarked that a person who destroys the works of man is condemned as a vandal, but a man who destroys the works of God is praised as a sportsman. I cannot even begin to understand how anyone, by use of dogs, gun or rod, can turn a thing of movement, life and beauty into a bloody bedraggled corpse, all in the name of pleasure. There might be some excuse if the animals were to be eaten, but, as it has been said, the fox hunt is "the unspeakable in pursuit of the uneatable."

It is one thing for a farmer to go out with a gun to find a hare for the pot: it is quite another thing to see an organised shoot where hundreds of game birds are shot merely for the pleasure of killing them. In my mind the life of a gamekeeper is a sad one; to spend the best part of a year rearing and nurturing his birds and then come October and November to have to beat them through the woods or over the hill to the gun.

The argument that hunting is a method of control is a nonsense, and those who propound that defence know it is a nonsense. Those who believe that the fox is not the villain he is so often painted, will find comfort in the winning essay in the fifth annual Kenneth Allsop Memorial Essay Competition. The winner, a shepherd who farms a large flock of blackface sheep on the hills above Loch Katrine in the West Highlands of Scotland, concludes his essay:

It will take much persuasion and education to replace old folklore with the knowledge that clean healthy ground and abundant grazing are enhanced by the 'Auld Enemy.' In the meantime I go on my rounds herding my sheep, and very welcome is the sight of my friend the fox[5].

The attitude of those who hunt was best summed up for me by a letter quoted in the *Sunday Times* and addressed to members of the hunt by a Master of Otterhounds:

The going is tough, but that is nothing new in our daily lives. Of course our sport is affected like everything else, but if we really value it we will fight hard to preserve our *pleasure*. Hunting is one of those rare things that allows the British to express their freedom, which is why those who wish to *sell us into bondage* encourage the uncommitted to attack it[6].

7

The living bodies of animals, including the human animal, have been used throughout the ages in the search for knowledge, in an attempt to wrest from their bodies the secrets of nature[7]. The earliest records of such work come from the Alexandrian school of vivisection in 330 B.C. Later, in 130 A.D. Galen was accused of experimenting on human beings as well as on swine. Shakespeare makes Cornelius, the doctor in *Cymbeline*, repudiate the Queen's suggestion to try the effect of drugs on animals:

Your highness
Shall from this practice but
Make hard your heart;
Besides the seeing these
Effects will be
Both noisome and infectious.

The Italian vivisection school flourished in the Middle Ages, but the animal experimentation cults in France and Germany did not develop fully until about the middle of the nineteenth century. Their experimental work on animals was the beginning of modern vivisectional methods on which, rightly or wrongly, modern medicine is based with its emphasis on drug therapy[8].

The word "vivisection," although its strict meaning is "to cut while alive," has come to mean any experiment or procedure performed on a living animal which is not for the benefit of that animal. The use of animals for experiments "calculated to cause pain" is governed in Great Britain by the *Cruelty to Animals Act, 1876*. At the time this piece of legislation was enacted, there were some three hundred and fifty experiments a year on animals. These were medical experiments, mainly in the fields of physiology or anatomy. The same Act now has to cope with over five million experiments annually, many of them of little or no genuine medical value. As the Houghton/Platt Memorandum puts it:

The catalogue of mutilation, misery, downright cruelty to animals in experiments is both lengthy and horrifying. The public believes that all experiments are conducted for medical research. They do not realise that the use of animals has spread into cosmetics, testing of weedkillers, detergents, soaps, into university departments of psychology, zoology, ecology, forestry and agriculture[9].

8

Although I have worked professionally in animal welfare for many years and my specialised field is the use of animals for research, I am still horrified when I read in the scientific press of the monstrous crimes that scientists all over the world commit against the animal creation for the most trivial of reasons.

Dr Donald Gould, writing in the *General Practitioner* on experiments performed in America by Dr R. J. White of the Metropolitan Hospital in Cleveland, who isolated the still living brains of monkeys, asked if such living brains could experience pain, fear, frustration, anger or dread: "After all, an isolated brain can't scream, or weep or bare its teeth." Dr White's work has now progressed to grafting whole monkey heads onto the necks of other monkeys. Dr Gould could see nothing of the smallest use to the practising physician or to people suffering from disorders of the brain or mind that has emerged from these horrific experiments but he warns:

> If we don't retain the utmost respect for life in all its forms, and if we don't recognise the heavy responsibility arising from the *de facto* domination which we indeed have over every living thing that moveth upon the earth, then the benefits to mankind which may flow from animal experiments will, in the end, prove to be of small account[10].

It is not only in the USA that such things happen. In a unique trial at a sheriff court in Scotland in 1978, a senior lecturer at St. Andrews University, one of the oldest seats of learning in Scotland, was convicted under the *Protection of Animals (Scotland) Act, 1912* "in that he did cruelly ill-treat, torture or terrify 178 canaries, 160 laboratory mice, 17 goldfish and 2 rats." The lecturer had been responsible for supervising experiments into the play behaviour and prey-catching ability of the domestic feline and permitted the canaries, mice, rats and goldfish to be used as live prey in the experiments which were conducted at the University over a period of a year.

In an article in the *Scotsman*, Dr Alice Heim, a leading Cambridge scientist and President of the Psychological Section of the British Association for the Advancement of Science, was reported as giving at the Association's annual conference, examples of psychological experiments which demanded "the infliction of severe deprivation or abject terror or inescapable pain—either mental or physical":

Rats drowning in a tank after being left to swim for 80 to 90 hours *to explore differences in the "will to live"*;

Baby rabbits dying of burst bladders after being taken from the mother before she could lick their ducts clean *in an experiment on "maternal affection"*;

Young monkeys and their mothers separated in anguish *to test "maternal deprivation."*

She accepted that such research would indubitably add to our knowledge, but it is obtained at a high price in mental and physical suffering[11].

In Scotland, the Agricultural Research Council have been conducting experiments into "the effects of breed, birthcoat and bodyweight on the cold resistance of newborn lambs." Ninety five lambs of different breeds, aged between six hours and seventy five hours old were taken from their mothers for one experiment. Some of the lambs were close-clipped (leaving about 2mm wool) and then placed in a climate chamber at a temperature of 36°C. After an hour the temperature in the chamber was lowered to freezing point then further lowered to reach minus 12°C. Finally it was lowered to 20 degrees of frost. In addition, some lambs were subjected to wind exposure.

The conclusion reached from these experiments, as published in a scientific journal was: "The experiments show that resistance of lambs to cold exposure in a climate chamber is influenced by breed, birthcoat and birthweight".[12] I would have thought that any good hill shepherd could have reached this conclusion without using a considerable sum of taxpayer's money (one newspaper report put the cost at twenty thousand pounds per annum) or without inflicting such unnecessary suffering on new born lambs.

How many experiments of the 5,195,409 performed in Britain in 1978 (the most recent Home Office annual return)[13] were unjustifiable in terms of animal suffering? The animal welfare societies can certainly quote many examples of useless and wasteful experiments and the annual return, which can hide more information than it reveals, reports that, amongst others, 28,238 experiments were performed during the year to test cosmetics; 14,892 to test household substances; 69,207 to test weedkillers. A further 91,076 experiments were undertaken in behavioural research, a few examples of which were described by Dr Heim.

The Sensitive Scientist, a report by a British Association study group commented:

Painful experiments on animals can be justified, but only if the benefits from them are correspondingly large, and those benefits cannot be obtained in any other more acceptable way. . . .

. . . However great the anticipated benefits, there may be some experiments which cannot be justified under any circumstances[14].

Other forms of abuse

This chapter has only skimmed the surface of what is done to animals. The list is virtually endless. Wild animals, creatures of the jungle and desert, creatures of the night and those from the frozen wastes, are all incarcerated in zoos and wildlife parks. (Those who think all is well in such places should read the book by Bill Jordan and Stefan Ormrod, *The Last Great Wild Beast Show*.)[15] Performing animals in circuses and films are subject to indignity and close confinement, even if cruelty in training cannot be proved. The light at the end of the tunnel for these animals is the dwindling number of travelling circuses and the refusal of many local authorities to allow circuses on municipally owned land.

The world of horses, particularly in regard to the growing trade for slaughter for the table, also involves suffering. Conditions in auctions and sale rings are only a few of the matters of concern in this very professional area of exploitation. Pet animals too, are often made to suffer. The mutilation of pedigree dogs, either through intensive breeding or by surgical means, to fit in with what man thinks a breed should look like, frequently results in a lifetime of misery for the animal.

It is a distressing fact that over two thousand dogs are destroyed every single day of the week in this country, simply because there are just too many dogs.[16] Many pet owners will not or cannot be bothered to prevent their dogs producing unwanted litters by having their bitches spayed. This is even more the case with cat owners. The argument that it is going against nature to prevent animals having young conveniently overlooks the fact that when man first took the dog and the cat into his home, he went against nature in removing these animals from the more natural controls on their species (predators, weather, food supply and disease).

What we may do to animals in the future

At a conference on animal potential held in Paris in the summer of 1978, scientists from all over the world discussed research projects aimed at creating super-intelligent animals. Already in Russia and the USA pigeons have been used to replace humans on the factory assembly line: trained birds have been used by an American pharmaceutical firm to sort out faulty drug capsules, but the birds were got rid of when the unions theatened to take the employers to court. In Russia such problems do not hinder the development of animal potential. A new pigeon takes only three or four days to train and has better eyesight than a man and can therefore detect smaller flaws in machinery parts.

One of the experts in this field, a Dr Kropivny, is reported as having informed the conference that in the future it is by no means impossible that chimps could do almost all the housework in hospitals, hostels and even private homes. He was not talking in terms of a hundred years into the future—but of what might happen *during the next decade.*

We have a new slave race in the making, one with no rights and no voice to protest, which makes the need for action in the field of animal welfare and protection vitally necessary. All of us working in any capacity at all in animal welfare have the responsibility squarely on our shoulders. If we fail, those who will follow us will condemn us because our energies are all too often devoted to fighting each other rather than the common enemy.

CHAPTER II

THE ANIMAL SOCIETIES—
"WHERE DID THEY ALL COME FROM"?

The history of the animal welfare movement is part of the history of a larger movement seeking humane reform which has been one of the driving forces in the history of mankind. Anthony Brown, who wrote the history of the RSPCA to mark the 150th Anniversary of that organisation, points out that whilst five thousand animals could be slaughtered in one day to please the crowd at the games in ancient Rome, there were those who rejected such needless slaughter:

> The story of humane reform is, above all, the story of those who refused to acquiesce. Even in the heyday of Imperial Rome there were a handful of such spirits. There was Cicero, who asked what pleasure an educated man could have in seeing a fine animal run through with a spear? There was Plutarch, the historian, who would not allow his old oxen to be slaughtered but put them out to grass instead. Years ahead of his time, he wrote pamphlets attacking not only hunting but the practice of starving animals before their death to make the meat taste better.[1]

That same spirit of refusing to acquiesce is what drives people today from different walks of life to fight against injustice wherever they find it. Often opposing the orthodox and established view, they will fight and keep on fighting against overwhelming odds until they win. The abolition of the slave trade is perhaps one of the best examples of this, especially as that battle has many similarities to the present campaign to gain rights for other "lesser" species—the animals.

Britain in the reign of George III was little better than Imperial Rome as far as the lot of animals was concerned. A. W. Moss, a former Secretary of the RSPCA, describes the scene in England at that time in his book *Valiant Crusade*:

> It was no unusual happening for a horse to be beaten to death;

13

whilst bull-baiting, bear-baiting and cock-fighting had again become popular entertainment in towns and villages alike. Fights were arranged between dogs and cats, or dogs and monkeys, and a delighted audience roared its approval as the stronger of the two animals tore his adversary to pieces and stood triumphant over a mangled heap of blood and fur. Cattle, sheep and pigs brought to London for slaughter were killed in underground cellars, the sheep being literally thrown out of the carts, where the animals lay bruised and injured for days at a time, until finally put out of their misery by the slaughterer's knife. Calves were strung up, their mouths taped to still their cries and were slowly bled to death.[2]

Before we congratulate ourselves by saying, "Well at least things are much better now—even if they are not perfect," we might well consider what Doris Rybot says in her book, *It Began before Noah*:

We should be very chary of condemning the pitiless brutality of our forefathers. Our own hands are not clean. We may have many laws now protecting animals; for all that, modern man, in the high cold names of Science and Medical Research submits creatures to, certainly very different cruelties, but nonetheless cruelties beside which many early and medieval torments pale.[3]

However, consciences were beginning to stir. Not surprisingly the Quakers were the first to speak out, led by George Fox, and they were followed by the Methodists and later by the established Church. Writers and artists including such illustrious figures as Blake, Cowper, Wordsworth, Burns, Browning and Hogarth, who penned the famous series of cartoons, *The Four Stages of Cruelty*, also made a stand against the obvious cruelties of the day.

In April 1800, Sir William Pulteney sought leave in the House of Commons to introduce a Bill to ban bull-baiting. The Bill was defeated by only two votes. The *Times* of 25th April 1800 was explicit on the matter:

It should be written in letters of gold that a government cannot interfere too little with the people; that laws, even good ones, cannot be multiplied with impunity, and whatever meddles with the private personal disposition of a man's time or property—is tyranny direct.

14

Legislation to ban bull-baiting was not successful until 1835, but in the meantime Lord Erskine of Restormel introduced a Bill to prevent malicious or wanton cruelty to horses, sheep and dogs. This Bill also failed on second reading, but a new champion had entered the lists, Richard Martin, Member of Parliament for Galway, who introduced a Bill to prevent the cruel and improper treatment of cattle. The Bill passed through the House of Commons, but was rejected by the Lords. Undaunted, Martin reintroduced the Bill the following year and with Lord Erskine to steer it through the House of Lords the Bill received the Royal Assent on the 22nd July 1822, and Richard Martin acquired a new nickname—"Humanity Dick."

Two years later, the Reverend Arthur Broome called a meeting which was attended by a number of eminent people, including Richard Martin and the man who had been largely responsible for abolishing slavery, William Wilberforce. This meeting was held to discuss the protection of animals and at it the RSPCA came into existence. Arthur Broome became the Secretary of the Society and in the minute book, which is still preserved, it is recorded that two committees were appointed. One was to superintend "the publication of tracts, sermons and similar modes of influencing public opinion." The other was concerned with inspecting markets and the streets of the metropolis, the slaughterhouses and "the conduct of coachmen."

It is generally thought that the RSPCA, which incidentally received its Royal Charter in 1840 from Queen Victoria, is the oldest animal welfare society in the world. In fact, this distinction belongs to the Liverpool Society for Preventing Wanton Cruelty to Brute Animals, which was instituted on 25th October 1809. The Liverpool Society later became the Liverpool branch of the RSPCA.

In 1836, the Belfast SPCA was founded by a retired naval officer, Commander Francis Calder. The name of the Society was changed in 1891 to the name by which we know it today, The Ulster Society for the Prevention of Cruelty to Animals. Scotland came next, when, according to a newpaper report, "a numerous and highly respectable public meeting" was held in Edinburgh on 18th December 1839. An independent society was inaugurated in Glasgow in 1856, which was followed by the formation of similar organisations in Dundee in 1864 and Aberdeen in 1870. This situation, with four separate organisations covering Scotland has prevailed to the present day, apart from the amalgamation of the Dundee SPCA with the Scottish SPCA in Edinburgh.

Branches of these organisations in England and Scotland were being formed at this time and, in addition, a number of societies were being formed in Ireland. It is perhaps interesting to note that one of the pioneer humane societies in Ireland, the Cork SPCA founded in 1879 by John Newsom, had as its motto: "We speak for those who cannot speak for themselves"—almost certainly the origin of this well-known phrase.

In 1860 a Mrs Tealby and a Mrs Major started a fund for a dogs' home as a result of seeing the miserable state of a half-starved stray. This home which was established in spite of the jeers of the *Times*, opened its doors at premises in Holloway. Today the Home for Lost and Starving Dogs is at Battersea.

It was now the turn of the growing anti-vivisection movement to establish itself. Although there had been agitation in Parliament and on the part of the RSPCA, the anti-vivisection campaign really started at an afternoon tea-party held at a villa at Bellosguardo in Florence, the same villa which had stirred the poet Robert Browning to write some of his finest poetry. One of the guests, Miss Cobbe, who was staying at the villa, listened over tea to a Dr Appleton describing a visit he had paid to Professor Schiff's laboratory. E. Douglas Hume describes the scene vividly in his book, *The Mind-Changers*:

> And then all was changed. The sky above seemed to be darkened; below, the glamour to fade from the fairylike city. It was a hell, still.[4]

Frances Power Cobbe had already had an article published in *Fraser's Magazine, The Rights of Man and the Claims of Brutes*, and as a result of that afternoon's gathering, she was to ensure that the cries of the laboratory animal would echo around the world. She worked initially through the RSPCA, but decided after the setting up of the first Royal Commission on Vivisection that a separate organisation was needed to fight the vivisectors. The first meeting of the new society was held on 2nd December 1875, at the home of Drs George and Frances Hogan, a married couple who were both doctors of medicine. In this way the first specialised

16

society concentrating on one field of exploitation was formed. The following March the Society for the Protection of Animals Liable to Vivisection took offices in Victoria Street, Westminster, and became known as the Victoria Street Society, the society which was eventually to change its name to the National Anti-Vivisection Society (NAVS).

Other anti-vivisection societies were being formed, notably the London Anti-Vivisection Society in 1876 (eventually amalgamating with the NAVS), and the World League Against Vivisection in 1898, the organisation responsible through Miss Margaret E. Ford for inaugurating "World Day of Prayer for Animals." The Scottish Anti-Vivisection Society was also founded in 1876 as the Scottish Society for the Total Suppression of Vivisection, as was the Society for United Prayer for the Prevention of Cruelty to Animals Especially with Regard to the Practice of Vivisection, which subsequently shortened it rather cumbersome title to the Society of United Prayer for Animals.

My own society, the Scottish Society for the Prevention of Vivisection, is a comparative newcomer and was originally founded as a branch of the NAVS. The Scots, however, being careful of sending their *sillar* over the border, resolved at the first general meeting to found the Scottish Co-operative Anti-Vivisection Society to take up the work of the Scottish branch of the National Anti-Vivisection Society. The following year the name was changed to the Scottish Society for the Prevention of Vivisection. It is interesting to note that at that first meeting held in Edinburgh on 21st December 1911, the annual subscription to the Society was set at five shillings and it remains the same to the present day, with our current subscription of twenty-five pence.

Miss Cobbe remained active in the Victoria Street Society until 1897, when a disagreement with a newly appointed Secretary of the Society, the Honourable Stephen Coleridge, led to a deep rift between herself and the Society. The latter had decided to "seek lesser measures" to check abuses, with prohibition not as an immediate but as an ultimate aim. She wrote bitterly in her autobiography:

> I and all the oldest members of the Victoria Street Society sorrowfully withdrew from what we had proudly but very mistakenly called 'our' Society.[5]

17

In 1898, Miss Cobbe founded the British Union for the Abolition of Vivisection at Bristol, with her ideal of total abolition written firmly into its constitution. John Vyvyan in his history of the anti-vivisection movement writes:

> The fragmentation of this great movement was a tragic event. It may have been inevitable, but that does not make it less sad. . . .
> . . . the old unity of purpose had been replaced by dissension, and the cause had received a long festering wound.[6]

Other specialist societies were now being formed. The National Canine Defence League was formed in 1891, and at the turn of the century the Feline Defence League, which later merged with the RSPCA came into existence. In 1927 the Cats Protection League was established, and the Peoples' Dispensary for Sick Animals of the Poor opened its first treatment centre in a cellar in Whitechapel in London in 1917. The PDSA's founder, Mrs Dickin, had seen the pitiful state of animals during the eighteen years she had worked with children in the slums.

In 1889, a Mrs Williamson living near Manchester founded among her personal friends and acquaintances a Society for the Protection of Birds. After two years hard work she transferred the Society to London. The first annual report of the Society was published in 1891 and the balance sheet recorded income of £7.13.8d. and expenditure at £6.3.11¼d. The Society in 1904 was granted a Royal Charter and became the Royal Society for the Protection of Birds.

The Animal Defence Society, which played a large part in humane slaughter reform and was responsible for setting up a model slaughterhouse at Letchworth, was founded in 1906 through the work of Miss Lind-af-Hageby and Nina, Duchess of Hamilton and Brandon, both of whom were closely connected with my own society. In 1926, as a result of the Anti-Steel-Toothed Trap Committee and the work of the National Council for Animals' Welfare, Major C. W. Hume founded the University of London Animal Welfare Society, now known as the Universities Federation for Animal Welfare (UFAW). The National Equine Defence League, which was also founded at this time, was responsible for the appointment of a Royal Commission which led to the passing of legislation for the protection of animals working underground.

The need for such protection may not be understood today, but in the ten years from 1920 to 1930, excluding 1926, a strike year, *85,372 pit ponies were killed or injured*. The earliest of the horse societies was the Home of Rest for Horses, founded in 1886 by a Miss Lindo who gave tired London working horses a rest in a field at Neasden. The Home is now at Westcroft Stables, Aylesbury.

The close of the nineteenth century saw other new organisations. Around this time were formed our Dumb Friends' League (1887), later to become the Blue Cross, the Jack London Club (1914), now the Performing and Captive Animals Defence League, (the word "Captive" is now dropped from the title to avoid confusion with the Captive Animals' Protection Society formed in 1957), the Council of Justice to Animals and the Humane Slaughter Association (1928) formed with the express purpose of combating slaughterhouse evils. In 1924, Mr Ernest Bell established the League for the Prohibition of Cruel Sports. E. Douglas Hume comments that "unfortunately, stormy times arose within the League, and some of the subsequent gatherings were noisier than any meet of the fox-hounds". From such meetings arose the second society dealing with hunting, the National Society for the Abolition of Cruel Sports.

In 1923 Mrs Kate Hosali, known as Toubiba (Arabic for lady Doctor), and her daughter Nina started the Society for the Protection of Animals in North Africa. This was the first of the societies established to seek funds and gain protection for animals overseas. There are now many such organisations, the Brooke Hospital for Animals in Cairo, the Anglo-Italian, the Anglo-Spanish and the Anglo-Venetian Societies, the Greek and the Japan Animal Welfare Societies and the Society for Animal Welfare in Israel.

Another group of societies are those with a religious base. Among these are the Friends' Anti-Vivisection Association (1897) later renamed the Friends' Animal Welfare and Anti-Vivisection Society and now known as Quaker Concern for Animal Welfare; the Catholic Study Circle for Animal Welfare founded in 1935,(although their first meetings as a group to organise united prayer for animals date from 1929); and the latest of these societies, the Anglican Society for the Welfare of Animals, formed in 1970.

This outline of the animal societies in Britain cannot list all the organisations and the many people who have devoted their lives to this cause; their number is legion. Since the early days of the movement, many new societies have been established to deal with new situations and new forms of exploitation which have arisen. Examples of these are the organisations concerned with farm animals, the Dartmoor Livestock Protection Society and Compassion in World Farming being two of the best known. Beauty Without Cruelty was founded by Lady Dowding to draw attention to the cruelties in the world of beauty and furs. The Fund for the Replacement of Animals in Medical Experiments (FRAME) was established to publicise the use of humane alternative methods of research and there are also the many funds and trusts set up to provide financial support for such research. Of course, this list is far from complete, as there are many smaller or local animal welfare societies, as well as the countless sanctuaries and refuges, ranging from the Wood Green Animal Shelter in London (1924) to the Lothian Cat Rescue in Scotland (1979).

Doris Rybot makes the point in *It Began Before Noah:*

> This road we have trod with the beasts is a long road, a bloody road, and the end of vileness is not yet in sight. For all that, it is a road lit always by the few in every generation who have loved, marvelled, cared and made true friendships with the beasts.

What used to be a few people in every generation is now swelling into a great tide, which one hopes will continue to flood until animals are granted those rights which never could have been denied them "but by the hand of tyranny."

CHAPTER III

CHARITY LAW AND THE ANIMAL WELFARE SOCIETIES

There can be no doubt that the question of charity status has a decisive effect on the work of societies. Most people probably think of animal welfare societies as charitable, but some societies are not charities, that is, registered charities recognised by the Charity Commissioners in England and Wales and the Inland Revenue in Scotland. One may feel this is not a matter of any great importance, but it is of considerable relevance to the societies for two quite separate reasons. It is also important that the public, and in particular those who give support to the work of the societies, understand the problems related to charitable status.

Being a registered charity confers upon an organisation not merely a status symbol and a cloak of respectability, but exemption from payment of income, capital gains and corporation taxes. It is therefore a financial inducement to any organisation involved in helping others, either in a practical way or by reform of social, ethical or moral conditions.

The law on charities, however, is very vague. It is based on a Preamble to an Act passed during the reign of Queen Elizabeth I in 1601,[1] a Preamble which itself was based on even earlier material which can be traced back to *Piers Plowman* in the 14th Century. A Charity is to:

> amend mesondioux therewith: and miseased folk helpe: and wicked ways wightly amend: and do bote to bridges that to-broke were: Marry maidens, or make them nuns: Poor people and prisoners, find them food: and set scholars to school, or to some other crafts: Relieve (men of) religion and rent them better.[2]

The Elizabeth I Preamble developed the application of charitable funds to achieve, for example, "the repair of bridges, ports, havens, causeways, churches, sea-banks and highways" (to use modern language), but basically the classifications remained the same and indeed they remain so to the present day. For practical

21

purposes the courts have for many years accepted the classification of charities made by Lord M'naghten in 1891:

"Charity" in its legal sense comprises four principal divisions: trusts for the relief of poverty; trusts for the advancement of education; trusts for the advancement of religion; and trusts for other purposes beneficial to the community not falling under any one of the preceding heads.[3]

Anti-vivisection societies, in common with other animal welfare organisations, enjoyed full charitable status until 1947. In that year, as a result of a letter to the *Times* by the Research Defence Society asking for an enquiry as to why anti-vivisection funds and income did not attract tax, the anti-vivisection societies were declassified on appeal to the House of Lords (*The National Anti-Vivisection Society v the Inland Revenue Commissioners,* 1948 AC.31). The societies were declassified as charities on the following grounds:

1. That the abolition of vivisection so far from being for the public benefit was gravely injurious thereto; and
2. A society which has as one of its principal objectives the promotion of a change in the law cannot be charitable.

This has since been clarified by the Report of the Charity Commissioners 1969, under the heading *Political Activities by Charities.* The report says:

It is a well established principal of Charity Law that a trust for the attainment of a political object is not a valid charitable trust and that any purpose with the object of influencing the legislature is a political purpose. Thus no organisation can be a charity and at the same time include among its purposes the object of bringing influence to bear directly or indirectly on Parliament to change the general law of the land.[4]

This ruling applies to all charities including those working for the alleviation of human suffering, and in 1972 the Charity Commissioners warned "War on Want" that an advertisement placed by them in the *Times* was, in the opinion of the Commissioners, a breach of the law. The advertisement, which cost two thousand pounds, urged sympathisers of Bangladesh to send telegrams to a Member of Parliament in support of an emergency motion he had tabled.[5]

The decision on appeal in the case of the anti-vivisection societies was not unanimous and Lord Porter did not accept the view of the other Law Lords. In his dissenting judgement he stated that he could not accept that the anti-slavery campaign, or the enactment of the Factory Acts, or the abolition of the use of boy labour to sweep chimneys would be charitable only if those who supported such reforms did not advocate a change in the law.[6]

Major reforms almost invariably require legislation. This attitude, therefore, resulting from the decision in the case of the anti-vivisection societies, must in the long-run hinder if not defeat the objective of many charities—which is legislative reform—unless they sacrifice their charitable status.

I mentioned that there were two reasons for the importance of charity status. The first of these is obviously the financial consideration. The second, however, may not be immediately obvious, although I have mentioned it above. If animal welfare societies are registered charities, they must of necessity be continuously aware of the limitations imposed upon their work. Reference to political activity in such things as propaganda, advertising and contact with government departments or Members of Parliament, must be carefully monitored. Frequently such restraint is misunderstood by the public and supporters alike, as being a lack of punch and action in the campaigns conducted by certain societies.

The House of Commons Select Committee on Expenditure reviewed the question of charity law and the work of the Charity Commissioners in 1974, commenting on the limitations imposed on organisations by this rule. Some of the Committee's remarks relate to an issue in which I was personally involved:

> To take a recent example of their attitude, the Commissioners refused to accept, from the Organising Committee for Animal Welfare Year 1976 who are seeking charitable status for their organisation, the inclusion of the following among the objects of association. . . .

The wording the Commissioners objected to was contained in the objectives for Animal Welfare Year, which had been intended by

23

the Organising Committee to be as hard-hitting as possible. The original wording was as follows (the amended wording accepted by the Commissioners will be found in chapter five):

The arousal of a determination on the part of the public to take prompt and decisive action to end the ill-treatment of animals whether such action is to be of a positive nature or of a more direct nature e.g. action to encourage legislation for the increased protection, preservation and care of all animal life.[7]

The Expenditure Committee also agreed with Lord Porter's dissenting judgement and recommended new legislation to permit political activity in pursuit of a charitable objective, so long as it remains subordinate to the main purpose of the charity. Since then the Goodman Committee has made a similar recommendation.[8]

These reports were published in 1975 and 1976 respectively, but a government has yet to act on these recommendations. In the meantime, the anti-vivisection societies can engage in as much political activity as they wish—but they pay very heavily for the privilege.

CHAPTER IV

THE LAW AND ANIMAL WELFARE

It is said that "the law is an ass" and whether or not you believe this to be true, it does not alter the fact that protection for animals [1] must initially stem through the law, that is through legislation enacted by Parliament.

I would be the first to accept that legislation alone is not enough; legislation without education will not prevent acts of cruelty even when punishable in law. The use of the gin-trap in Scotland, for example, was banned from 1st April 1973 by the *Agriculture (Spring Traps) Scotland Act, 1969.* On 13th August 1979 a gamekeeper was fined two hundred and fifty pounds in Inverness Sheriff Court for setting in a tree a gin-trap which caught a golden eagle. The keeper's defence was that he had set the trap for wild-cats something which still would have been an offence under the 1969 Act. [2] The law did not stop him setting an illegal trap or from setting it in such a position as to catch a protected species. Only when education can bring about a change in attitude will much of the cruelty vanish.

The first attempt by Sir William Pulteney to introduce a Bill to ban bull-baiting came in 1800. The first successful Bill to prevent the cruel and improper treatment of cattle was the work of "Humanity Dick" Martin, Member for Galway, who was ably backed in the House of Lords by Lord Erskine of Restormel. This first Act for the protection of an animal received the Royal Assent on the 22nd July 1822. Prior to that date, animals had no protection in law, except perhaps as property. Yet it was possible for them to offend against the law. Animals were deemed to be responsible for their actions and could be brought to trial in a court of law, a custom which appears to have developed from the mediaeval ecclesiastical courts which took the injunction from the Book of Exodus which states: "if an ox gore a man or a woman, that they die; then the ox shall be surely stoned, and his flesh shall not be eaten; but the owner of the ox shall be quit." [3] It is probable that many thousands of pigs, dogs and cattle were tried and put to death as a result of this edict and, incredible as it may seem, such trials were held in Britain with the full panoply of the law. The animals accused of an offence had the same rights as an accused person and would appear in the dock and be defended by counsel who endeavoured to persuade the judge to acquit his client. The last such recorded trial in England was in 1771, when a dog was tried and convicted at Chichester in Sussex for killing a child.

Although animals were not given any protection under the law until 1822, there was a statute known as the "Black Act of 1722" (so nicknamed because of the penalties imposed on poachers with blackened faces),[4] which made certain acts unlawful. This Act rendered it a felony "unlawfully to kill, maim or wound any cattle." It was necessary, however, even when the most horrible cruelty had been displayed, *to prove malice against the owner*. In 1749, a case was brought against two men at Gloucester Assizes for killing a mare with a billhook to spite the owner; one of them received the death sentence.

Following Richard Martin's first success, bull-baiting, bear-baiting and cock-fighting were eventually outlawed in 1835, when Martin's Act was extended to include dogs and penalties were imposed for impounding or detaining animals without providing them with food. In 1839 the drawing of carriages, trucks and barrows by dogs was made illegal in the Metropolitan Police District. In 1849 (1850 in Scotland), an Act was passed which consolidated the earlier legislation and made the provisions more effective, and in 1854 the use of dogs to draw vehicles was abolished throughout the United Kingdom, protection being granted to "all domestic animals of any kind of species and whether quadrupeds or not."[5]

The first wild creatures to receive protection were seabirds. The *Sea Birds Protection Act, 1869* provided a close season for certain birds, but again not for the sake of the birds but in the interests of the farmers, the merchant seamen and the deep-sea fishermen who all suffered from a drop in the numbers of seabirds. Farmers were included because there were fewer birds following the plough, fishermen because gulls hovering over a shoal of fish made their task easier, and seamen because in foggy weather the cries of the gulls indicated the proximity of the shore. The Member who introduced the Bill, quoted statistical evidence to show that with the decrease in gulls, the number of ships going aground at Flamborough Head had increased.

It is interesting and important to note that amid all the accepted cruelties of that time, which were only just beginning to receive the attention of Parliament, vivisection, the use of living animals for experimentation, was the subject of the next legislation in the *Cruelty to Animals Act, 1876*. Since all the earlier Acts have been incorporated in the *Protection of Animals Acts* of 1911 and 1912, the *Cruelty to Animals Act* enjoys the doubtful distinction of being the oldest animal welfare legislation remaining on the statute book. It was on this peg that the Animal Welfare Year campaign was hung.

I have already given some of the background to the anti-vivisection campaign in this country which led to the founding of the first "specialist" society, the Victoria Street Society, but it may be useful at this point to delve a little more deeply into what actually happened when Lord Carnarvon's Bill, designed to protect laboratory animals, was mutilated during its passage through Parliament.

Lord Carnarvon's granddaughter, the Hon Juliet Gardner, was a life member of the Scottish Society for the Prevention of Vivisection until her death in 1976, and in an historical note on the 1876 Act which she gave to the Society, she provided a detailed account of the happenings of that time:

Certain misunderstandings seem to have arisen with regard to the basic views held by my grandfather (Lord Carnarvon) in connection with the inception of the *Cruelty to Animals Act, 1876*. The title of the Act clearly indicates that the prime intention was to prevent cruelty to animals.

My grandfather and his brothers and sisters were convinced that the case against vivisection played a vital part in social progress, and in the ultimate emancipation of a great spiritual freedom founded on justice and compassion to our younger brethren.

One of his brothers, Mr Auberon Herbert, a Radical M.P., fought powerfully for the animals inside and outside the House of Commons. When the Report of the Royal Commission on Vivisection was published on 20th March 1876, Lord Shaftesbury headed a deputation to the Home Office, and

27

"urged the Government to bring in a Bill in accordance with the recommendations of the Commission." The deputation was very favourably received, and was asked to submit suggestions. Earlier, at Highclere Castle, the subject was much discussed, and Mr Auberon Herbert, M.P. approached Mr Delane, then Editor of the *Times* and whose sympathies were well known, to know if he would publish a letter on the subject.

Mr Delane's reply was very clear. He said that if (as Mr Auberon Herbert had promised) the letter was "very violent, very abusive, very extreme," he would have much pleasure in publishing it! Mr Auberon Herbert's letter filled nearly two columns in the *Times* of 17th January 1876. On its appearance and a later article written by an opponent of Mr Herbert's views, Lord Carnarvon wrote at once from the Colonial Office (he was Secretary for the Colonies) to his brother, saying, "I like your letter very much—and the article in today's *Times* shows that it has hit the mark"!

On 22nd May 1876, when Lord Carnarvon introduced the Bill, he was most unfortunately called away to the bedside of his mother, who died a few days later.

On 3rd June 1876, Queen Victoria, who abominated vivisection, wrote and condoled with him; her letter continued, "in the midst of his sorrow she knows that his heart will be with his work," and the Queen then went on to refer to "the horrible, disgraceful and un-Christian vivisection." The Duke of Richmond and Gordon wrote Her Majesty a letter, and she asked Lord Carnarvon "to communicate to him her very strong views on the subject." Lord Carnarvon hastened to reply that his heart did remain with his work.

It should be remembered that before this Bill was introduced, there had been great agitation about the evils of vivisection in this country, and the terrible accounts from abroad of experiments on live animals, and with no legislation or restriction whatsoever, caused all right-thinking people to hope that in this country vivisection would not assume an uncontrolled momentum. Meanwhile, in the background some doctors who favoured uncontrolled experimentation were loud in their criticism of Lord Carnarvon's proposals. In answer to their intervention, Mr Auberon Herbert was prophetic in the view which he expressed as to the deep underlying aim of his brother's Bill, namely, to meet what was virtually "a revolt of a part of Science against the authority of morality, and the pretension on her part to become an independent and sovereign State."

The medical lobby referred to was very powerful, as it is today, and as a result of the pressure it brought to bear on the Home Secretary, Mr R. A. Cross, he introduced a Bill altered to suit their demands. This was in the absence of and without the knowledge of Lord Carnarvon, the original sponsor of the Bill. This new Bill was rushed through and received the Royal Assent on 15th August 1876, only five days later, at the tail end of the session. No time was allowed for any real debate.

It is perhaps worth pondering on the fact that had Lord Carnarvon's Bill been enacted in its original form there would be no anti-vivisection movement in Britain today. Frances Power Cobbe records in her autobiography that under the provisions of Lord Carnarvon's Bill:

No experiment whatever under any circumstances was permitted on a dog, cat, horse, ass or mule; nor on any other animals *except under conditions of complete anaesthesia from beginning to end*. The Bill included licences, but no certificates dispensing with the above provisions. [6]

So called "cruel sports" came in for some attention at this time. Strange as it may seem today, pigeon shooting was the first sport to be tackled. Bills for the banning of this sport, which gave rise to extreme cruelty, were rejected by Parliament in 1882, 1883 and 1884. This is not surprising, when one considers that pigeon-shooting was a favourite pastime of members of both Lords and Commons. It was argued by a number of keen sportsmen that if pigeon-shooting were abolished it could lead to a demand for the banning of other field sports. History thus repeats itself.

Colonel King Harman was the most outspoken speaker. He said in the Commons that the Bill was "a precursor of legislation under which fishermen would be imprisoned, butchers hung and we should all be ridden over by rampant vegetarians." The shooting of captive pigeons released by hand, trap or other connivance was not banned until 1921, when public indignation over a shoot at Chatham Football Club forced Parliament to act.

A number of specialised Acts were passed at the turn of the century, [7] but the next major step forward was the *Protection of Animals Act, 1911* which A. W. Moss in *Valiant Crusade* referred to as the "sheet anchor of animal welfare." This Act was primarily a consolidating Act and was concerned with "the offence of cruelty." Apart from certain relatively minor amendments, this Act is the last one concerned with the offence of cruelty and it represents the current law on that subject.

The 1911 Act replaced the Acts of 1849 and 1854 together with the *Wild Animals in Captivity Act, 1900*, and incorporated two Acts of 1863 and 1864 dealing with the sale of poisoned grain and the placing of poisoned flesh. The core of the Act is in Section 1 which makes it an offence for any person to "cruelly beat, kick, ill-treat, over-ride, over-drive, over-load, torture, infuriate or terrify any animal." This section greatly extends the provisions of earlier legislation by making it an offence for any person to cause any unnecessary suffering to an animal, or, being the owner, to permit any unnecessary suffering by "wantonly or unreasonably doing or omitting to do any act, or causing or procuring the commission or omission of any act." There are two important innovations here; the causing of any unnecessary suffering is now an offence as well as the listed abuses, and, for the first time, the failure to prevent unnecessary suffering is an offence.

Although it was an important step forward in 1911, the phrase "unnecessary suffering" is a major problem to the animal welfare movement of today. If unnecessary suffering is an offence, then we must accept that there is such a thing as "necessary" suffering. The courts over the years have interpreted necessary suffering as "the balancing of the interests of man in the benefits of a particular course of action against the interests of the animal in freedom from suffering."

There are four exemptions to the 1911 Act: vivisection, the destruction of animals for food, wild animals (unless they can be classed as captive), and captive animals while they are being coursed or hunted. These then are four examples where the law considers suffering as being necessary; for the discovery of knowledge, for slaughter for food, and for the enjoyment of sport.

In the following year, the Act was extended to Scotland in the *Protection of Animals (Scotland) Act, 1912*. In that year the second Royal Commission on Vivisection, which had been deliberating since 1906 also completed its report. This had little effect on the use of animals for research, but it did have an unexpected result in the enactment of the *Animals (Anaesthetics) Act, 1919*[8] which required horses, dogs, cats and bovines to be under anaesthesia during painful operations.

Legislation from this time dealt in the main with special issues. One such piece of legislation was the *Dogs Act, 1906* which gave legal protection to strays and defined the liability of owners. Incidentally, this Act specifically precludes the handing over of strays (either giving or selling) for the purposes of vivisection. Other Acts relating to dogs are the *Diseases of Animals Act, 1950*, the *Breeding of Dogs Act, 1973* and more generally the *Pet Animals Act, 1951* which requires the licensing of pet shops. Similarly, the *Riding Establishments Acts, 1964 and 1970* and the *Animal Boarding Establishments Act, 1963*, require the licensing of such premises.

Farm animals are provided for in the *Agriculture Acts* and the *Agriculture (Miscellaneous Provisions) Acts*, in particular the *Miscellaneous Provisions Act, 1968*, which states:

Any person who causes unnecessary pain or unnecessary distress to any livestock for the time being situated on agricultural land and under his control or permits any such livestock to suffer any such pain or distress of which he knows or may be reasonably expected to know, shall be guilty of an offence.

Once again, the phrases "unnecessary pain" or "unnecessary distress" appear and this places the onus on the courts to decide what is "necessary." These Acts, as is the case with many others, have enabling clauses which permit the responsible minister to make regulations and orders. The orders made under one such Act, the *Diseases of Animals Act, 1950*, covered 1,595 pages of closely printed foolscap.

To list all the Acts that have come onto the statute book during this century would be superfluous, but I think three other Acts must be mentioned: the *Slaughterhouses Act, 1974*, which is the latest in a series of Acts on the slaughtering of animals for food, the

Veterinary Surgeons Act, 1966, and the *Protection of Birds Act, 1954*, which provides another good example of "necessary" suffering. The Act makes it an offence to "keep or confine any bird whatsoever in any cage or other receptacle which is not sufficient in height, length and breadth to permit the bird to stretch its wings freely." Immediately below this humane requirement, it is stated: *"providing this sub-section shall not apply to poultry."*

In addition, there have been a number of conservation measures which Parliament has considered from time to time. The earliest of these are the game laws, originally dating from 1427, which lay down close seasons for game. Richard Ford, to whom I am indebted for much of the factual information on legislation in this chapter, in his thesis *"The Law on Cruelty to Animals"*[9] comments:

> The motive for conservation of any creature is based almost entirely on concern for the interests of mankind either in the area of commerce, as in the 1869 Act; sport, as in the Game Acts which are concerned to preserve animals for sporting purposes or aesthetics as in the Protection of Birds Acts which are concerned to preserve species of birds for the spiritual satisfaction of Man. On the other hand the motive for protecting animals from cruelty is based almost entirely on a recognition and acceptance of the fact that man has duties towards animals and as a corollary of that acceptance, a concern to enforce those duties by law.

Recent Acts for the conservation of species include the *Deer (Scotland) Act, 1959*, the *Conservation of Seals Act, 1970*, the *Badgers Act, 1973*, and the *Conservation of Wild Creatures and Wild Plants Act, 1975*. It is on the schedule of protected animals under this last Act that the otter now receives protection in England and Wales, but not in Scotland, where its numbers are said to be plentiful. This is the basic difference between conservation and protection. Conservation is only concerned with numbers, whereas protection is concerned with the prevention of suffering.

There are many fascinating and often sad twists in the attitude of the law and the agencies which enforce it. The Scott-Henderson Committee's report in 1951, which led to the banning of the gin-trap in England and Wales under the *Pests Act, 1954*, (The use of the gin-trap was not banned in Scotland until 1973) defined the gin as "a diabolical instrument which causes an incalculable amount of suffering. Its sale and use in this country should be banned by law within a very short period of time."

In spite of that statement, the gin-trap is still manufactured in Great Britain today and we export this "diabolical instrument which causes an incalculable amount of suffering" to countries overseas. The Department of Trade has refused to consider banning such exports, on the basis that the trap may be used legally in many countries and Britain does not require goods which are exported from this country to conform with our regulations on such matters as health, safety and humanitarianism. One can only wonder whether we are also producing and exporting man-traps, thumb-screws and the like.

The legislation for the protection of animals has come a long way since the year 1800, but we still have a very long way to go before we obtain real protection for animals in law. This can only be achieved by changing the climate of public opinion and exerting sufficient pressure to force Parliament to act. If any illustration of the present state of the law is needed, one might ponder the jailing of two young Americans two or three years ago for releasing into the sea dolphins which were being used for research. Professor Meth of Seton Hall University commented:

> The law is concerned with prosecuting as criminals persons who released experimental-subject dolphins but the law will not ask by what right the scientists placed the dolphins in captivity in the first place.[10]

PART TWO

ANIMAL WELFARE YEAR

CHAPTER V

THE EARLY STRUGGLE

The planning for Animal Welfare Year started in the autumn of 1973, when the first germ of the idea was implanted in my mind at the Edinburgh Conference of Scottish Animal Welfare Societies. Following the conference, I had given a great deal of thought to the proposal for an animal welfare year which had been taken up by Mr F. A. Burden, from a suggestion made by Mr Christopher Mylne. The more I mulled it over in my mind, the more certain I became that this was the way forward. Looking back, I now know I was right, for despite all the problems and, at one time near disaster, the Year did succeed and was partly responsible for changing the animal welfare movement of this country.

The first step was to gain the approval of my own committee and the Board of Directors of the St. Andrew Animal Fund. Their response was to give me every encouragement, including a pledge to cover the cost of the salary for a paid organiser over a three-year period. It gives me great pleasure publicly to record my appreciation of my committee's confidence in me and their courage in embarking on such a mammoth undertaking, a step which very few committees if any would have been prepared to take.

It was clear that if such a national campaign was going to have any chance of success, I would have to have the support of the Royal Society for the Prevention of Cruelty to Animals, as this was the largest society in Britain. For this reason I wrote to Major R. F. Seager, who was then Executive Director of the RSPCA, requesting that he discuss the proposal for an Animal Welfare Year with his Council. As a result of this letter, I was invited to address the Executive and Finance Committee of the RSPCA, where I gave an outline of the proposal which had already received the enthusiastic support of the Scottish societies. Later on I provided a more detailed plan for the information of the Council at the request of the then Chairman, Mr J. S. Hobhouse, and for the first time I put a figure on what I considered would be the total cost of mounting such a campaign. The figure I quoted was fifty thousand pounds. As the Year's final accounts show the actual total expenditure amounted to £49,780.

I had at this time also been taking soundings from sympathetic Members of Parliament and the general view appeared to be that a national campaign of this kind would considerably strengthen the hand of the Parliamentary Animal Welfare Group in bringing pressure to bear on government for new legislation. The initial response from the RSPCA was somewhat disappointing. The Council approved the scheme in principle, but were not at that time, prepared to consider giving financial support. It must be remembered that at the end of 1974 the Society was faced with severe financial difficulties, not to mention the trauma of the panel of inquiry which was looking into the affairs and administration of the organisation. [1]

Time was beginning to run out and my chairman, Sir Gerald Reece, and I decided to go to Horsham and discuss the matter in person with Major Seager. We stressed the importance of RSPCA involvement and obviously the meeting had the desired effect since we were informed on 6th November that the Council had been receptive to our suggestion that, as a first step, we call a conference of all the animal societies in Britain to discuss the proposal and to gauge the volume of support for such a campaign.

On the 10th December 1974 the Royal Society for the Prevention of Cruelty to Animals and the St. Andrew Animal Fund jointly announced the proposal to designate 1976 as "Animal Welfare Year" (see Appendix A). The statement which was issued called upon all societies to discuss the proposals being put before them and to send a delegate to a one day exploratory conference to be held in London in February 1975. The statement concluded:

> If given sufficient support, "Animal Welfare Year" could be the major animal protection event of the century—if not of all time and the results could be more far-reaching than might be imagined. There can be no doubt that the attitude in Parliament is ready for a major reform of animal welfare legislation and it should not be forgotten that the echoes from "Animal Welfare Year" in Great Britain could well travel round the world.

The exploratory conference was held at the Kenilworth Hotel in

London, when forty-two societies were represented out of the seventy-nine organisations which had received the statement. A further twelve societies did not attend but indicated support.

As Chairman of the Conference, I was able to outline in more detail the proposal to launch Animal Welfare Year. I stressed that its aims were to:

1. Bring to the public's attention the considerable progress in animal welfare legislation which has taken place during the past hundred years.
2. Focus public attention on the present areas of concern and the likely developments in animal exploitation during the next hundred years unless adequate legislation was enacted.
3. Arouse sufficient public interest and concern during 1976, so that sympathetic M.P.'s could use such support in the future to urge government action to revise and bring up-to-date present legislation and for the introduction of new legislation.

Mr Burden, then spoke in support of the proposal urging all societies in Britain, whether or not they were represented at the Conference: "to give serious and urgent consideration to the proposal to designate 1976 as Animal Welfare Year." A general discussion followed on areas of concern which would form the basis for the Year's programme. In the course of the discussion these areas were identified:

PET ANIMALS— Stray, abandoned and unwanted dogs and cats; the importation of exotic animals as pets; and exotic animals in circuses, zoos, wildlife and safari parks; sporting animals (i.e. race horses, racing dogs etc.).

LABORATORY ANIMALS— Use of animals in non-medical research; the development of humane alternative methods of research; reforms in the administration of the *Cruelty to Animals Act 1876*.

FARM ANIMALS—	(including horses and ponies)—Access to intensive farm units; and access to riding and trekking establishments; assistance from the veterinary profession.
TRANSIT OF ANIMALS—	Tighter controls on all methods of shipment; the campaign against the export of food animals for slaughter.
GENERAL—	Performing animals (stage, circuses and films); hunting for sport.

The Conference also resolved to extend the areas of concern to include wild animals.

The moment of truth arrived after lunch, when I had to obtain a decision from the Conference as to whether or not we should proceed. I pointed out that funds to "prime the pump" were essential and apart from the St. Andrew Animal Fund, which had pledged up to nine thousand pounds to secure the salary of an organiser, the only society to make a pledge of financial support had been the Scottish Anti-Vivisection Society. This society had pledged five hundred pounds which from a small organisation represented a significant part of its income. If the fifty-four societies present or supporting the Year contributed a like sum this would provide initial funding of nearly thirty thousand pounds.

The Conference almost unanimously (the exception being the Universities Federation of Animal Welfare)[2] endorsed the proposal to designate 1976 as Animal Welfare Year, providing sufficient support was forthcoming when delegates reported back to their committees. One serious problem, however, did arise at this point. Although there was general agreement about holding the Year, a number of delegates expressed doubts as to whether there was sufficient time to prepare for the Year which was then less than ten months away. A little quick thinking solved this problem by deciding to date Animal Welfare Year from 15th August 1976, this being the anniversary of the date that the *Cruelty to Animals Act* received the Royal Assent. In this way we should be provided with an additional eight months for preparation. This decision, it subsequently transpired, had other advantages; Age Action Year was also being held in 1976, and by the time Animal Welfare Year was launched, Age Action Year had fired off most of its "big guns." 1977 was of course the Queen's Jubilee Year, and although this did have a marked effect on Animal Welfare Year, by that time we were well established.

The Conference elected the following people to serve on the Organising Committee for Animal Welfare Year:

Clive Hollands (SSPV)	- Laboratory animals
F. A. Burden, M.P.	- Parliament
D. Luetchford (RSPCA)	- General animal welfare
D. Whiting (BWC)	- Cosmetic experiments, fur-bearing animals
Mrs D. Hegarty (FRAME)	- Humane alternative methods of research
Col. A. H. Roosmalecocq, (NCDL)	- Pet animals
Arthur E. Parratt (CPL)	
Colin Platt (ISPA)	- Wild animals & international
Miss C. Hodgson (CSCAW)	- General animal welfare
J. A. C. Alexander-Sinclair (LACS)	- Cruelty to wild animals
Mrs G. Spooner (Ponies of Britain)	- Horses and ponies
Peter Roberts (CIWF)	- Farming

A report on the Conference was sent out to all societies and the first meeting of the Organising Committee was held in late February. It was at this meeting that I was formally elected Chairman. We decided that the Year must concentrate on clearly defined areas of animal exploitation where public interest and support might be forthcoming, and that with many organisations with differing viewpoints involved, controversial subjects must be avoided. The final agreed list of areas to be tackled was:

Farm Animals—	Mandatory codes of welfare for intensively farmed animals; slaughter of food animals; and the export of live animals for slaughter.

41

Laboratory Animals—	Use of animals in non-medical research; development of alternative methods of research; reforms in the administration of the *Cruelty to Animals Act, 1876.*
Pet Animals—	Stray, abandoned and unwanted animals; the responsibility of owners.
Wild Animals—	Endangered species; killing for commercial use; trapping for laboratories and placing on public show.

We resolved that publicity during Animal Welfare Year should avoid controversial issues and the accent should be on "realism" and not "idealism." I would like to pay tribute to the League Against Cruel Sports and their representative on the Organising Committee, Mr. John Alexander-Sinclair, since they not only accepted that the hunting issue was too controversial a matter to include in the Year's programme, but also decided to give their whole-hearted support to the campaign, a decision which is worthy of note and one which other societies could well emulate. It was agreed that at the May meeting of the Committee a final decision would be taken as to whether to proceed with Animal Welfare Year, depending on the total sum pledged by the societies. Other matters discussed concerned the appointment of a professional organiser, office accommodation, facilities for meetings, banking arrangements and the necessity of applying for charitable status.

This last matter was to bring me into contact with a charming character, a solicitor by the name of Neil Tosh, who was recommended to act for us in the matter of charitable status. Neil, in outlook, temperament, and indeed in every way, was as different from me as chalk is from cheese. Nevertheless we became firm friends and although he undertook the initial legal work of getting the Year off the ground on a professional basis, he later became Honorary Secretary of the company. This was largely, I like to think, because of our friendship.

A momentous meeting of the Organising Committee was held on 28th May, when the Committee were informed that of the ninety organisations approached fifty-three societies had pledged support for the campaign, twelve were opposed, nine had yet to hold committee meetings and sixteen had not replied. The total contributions pledged amounted to £23,846 and on this basis it was resolved:

That on the authority vested in the Organising Committee by the Exploratory Conference of 14th February 1975, and in view of the support now pledged by the Animal Welfare Societies of Britain, the proposal to designate 1976 as Animal Welfare Year is formally adopted.

The final list of societies supporting the Year appears in Appendix B.

Three important issues were taking up much of the time of the Committee at this point. Originally, we had considered drawing up a simple trust deed prior to registering as a charity, but because of a number of problems, one being personal and joint liability of trustees, we decided to register the Year as a company limited by guarantee and not having a share capital. Unfortunately this meant delays which resulted from discussions with the Board of Trade and the Registrar of Companies as well as with the Charity Commissioners. As already mentioned we experienced difficulty in agreeing suitable wording for the objects of the company which would be acceptable to us and the Commissioners.

Another matter was the question of organisation of the campaign. Our initial intention had been to appoint a professional organiser, but later we realised that other professional services would be required by the way of public relations and advertising. We therefore decided to pool all these requirements and appoint an agency to handle all aspects of the Year. We interviewed a number of such professional P.R. consultancies and advertising agencies and eventually selected the combined agency of Dexter, Brent and Paterson, and Infopress Limited. Fees for such professional services do not come cheap, but the Committee was impressed by the presentation of this agency and the fact that the agency was confident of being able to raise sufficient funds (in addition to the thirty thousand pounds we hoped the societies would contribute) to cover the costs of promoting the Year. This would be done by obtaining financial support from major companies, corporations, institutions and other organisations.

The final matter causing us concern was funds, as we were still short of over six thousand pounds on our target from the animal societies and we were particularly worried over the attitude of the RSPCA at this time as they had not yet undertaken to make a contribution. Only two months after the exploratory conference, I was informed that the Executive and Finance Committee did not consider that the aims of AWY, though laudable in themselves, represented a coherent programme upon which the Society could enter into any major financial commitment and it had been decided therefore that in the absence of any concrete proposals the RSPCA was unable to enter into any commitment at this time. There was nothing for it but once again to ask to speak to the Finance Committee or the full Council, which I did at the meeting of the full Council on 8th May 1975. The result of this was that Animal Welfare Year was given a grant of five thousand pounds from the RSPCA.

I had felt incidentally, that it was a little hard to accuse the Organising Committee of not having a "coherent programme" since we had had little time at that stage to even consider the programme. In addition to the other matters referred to earlier, we were involved in seeking royal patronage in the person of Prince Charles, and we were also approaching Lord Houghton of Sowerby to act as the Year's President. Others were being asked to serve as Vice-Presidents.

I was delighted when Lord Houghton accepted our invitation to become President, and since those far-off days we have worked closely together on a number of projects. The following also agreed to be Vice-Presidents of the Year:

Dr. Edward Carpenter, Dean of Westminster
A. Gwyn Benyon Esq.
The Dowager Duchess of Hamilton & Brandon
The Viscount Massereene and Ferrard
Lady Parker of Waddington
Sir Gerald Reece

Mr. Gwyn Benyon was a former Chief Veterinary Officer of the Ministry of Agriculture. Lady Parker, who had offered herself in place of the smoking beagles at the ICI laboratories, was a charming and fascinating person to whom I owe a tremendous debt of gratitude for her support and encouragement in those early days. Our occasional lunches together were a port of haven in what were very troubled and stormy waters. I was also very pleased that my own Chairman, Sir Gerald Reece, accepted a vice-presidency as I was when the Dowager Duchess of Hamilton and Brandon accepted the same post, as this was a direct link wih the family which had done so much in the early days of the movement, through Nina, Duchess of Hamilton and Brandon.

The Committee has been criticised for seeking royal patronage, first from Prince Charles, and subsequently by approaching Prince Philip and the Duchess of Kent, but it must be remembered that such patronage appeals to those from whom we were looking for financial support. We were not however successful in any of these attempts.

At the meeting at the end of September 1975, the new company, Animal Welfare Year, was incorporated. Before I stood down as Chairman of the Organising Committee, I thanked the members and stressed that there would have been insurmountable difficulties in coming this far had not the members of the Committee worked in close harmony. The formal business of complying with the requirements of the Companies Acts was quickly disposed of, including the appointment of the organising Committee as directors of the Company and myself as Chairman. The final agreed objective of Animal Welfare Year, as stated in the company's Memorandum and Articles of Association, was:

To prevent cruelty to animal life by the promotion of humane behaviour so as to reduce pain, fear and stress inflicted upon animals by mankind whether relating to pet animals, wild animals, animals used in laboratory experiments, farm animals, performing animals or any other form of animal life.

Time was pressing. At that meeting we also discussed the "logo" and slogan for the Year, which we had put out to a market research survey test to ascertain which of a number of choices had the most impact upon the public. The slogan chosen was "Our future is in Your Hands." (The logo is reproduced in Appendix C together with Lord Houghton's Introduction to the Business brochure).

At long last Animal Welfare Year was on the move and the animal societies were beginning to respond. Many of the societies could not afford to give large contributions; indeed some could not afford to make any financial contribution. The names of the societies which generously responded to the campaign must be recorded.

Beauty Without Cruelty (Scotland)	£1,000
British Union for the Abolition of Vivisection	500
Cats Protection League	500
Central Council for SPCA's in Scotland	500
Crusade Against All Cruelty to Animals	500
League Against Cruel Sports	500
Performing Animals Defence League	1,000
RSPCA	5,000
St. Andrew Animal Fund	9,000
Scottish Anti-Vivisection Society	500
Scottish Society for the Prevention of Vivisection	2,000
Whitley Animal Protection Trust	500

Other societies gave sums ranging from two hundred and fifty pounds to five pounds, and in this context one organisation must be specially mentioned. The Performing Animals Defence League wrote to us in April 1975, stating that the League would give every support to Animal Welfare Year. The letter continued:

We have given much thought to the amount of financial contribution we can make, for although we get through a considerable amount of work, our income from members' subscriptions and donations is very limited since many of them have been unable to increase their pre-1969 subscriptions of 25 pence per annum. Thus our total income averages only £1,500. However, so important do we consider Animal Welfare Year to be that we are prepared to initially guarantee two thirds of our income—i.e. £1,000. Should the fund require further contributions, we will do our best to comply.

Such a magnificent response was heart-warming, to say the least, and by the time the company was launched we believed we were on the road to success. But there were many disappointments still to come.

CHAPTER VI

And Some Fell on Stony Ground

A final total of sixty-seven animal welfare societies participated in Animal Welfare Year and, as an article in the *Spectator* put it, "the assortment of organisations joining in, from the Cats' Protection League to Compassion in World Farming, gives some clue to the medley of interests involved."[1] Unfortunately, for a variety of reasons a number of societies did not join in although they all made a point of praising the objectives of the Year and wishing us well. Nigel Sitwell, Director of Publicity for the World Wildlife Fund, for example, said that the WWF would prefer not to become actively involved, since it was felt that participation might blur identity and perhaps blunt their fund-raising edge. He assured us however that the WWF did not disagree with our general aims and wished the Year every success. A number of the organisations which did not participate took the view that supporting the Year would detract from their own society's fund-raising, whereas if the experience of my own society is anything to go by, we found greater interest, increased membership and improved fund-raising all resulted from the Year.

The National Anti-Vivisection Society refused our invitation to participate in the Year. This was a bitter blow to me, as the NAVS is an important society in its own right and I had believed that at least I would be able to count on the support of all the anti-vivisection societies. As soon as I received the letter from the NAVS conveying the decision of their council, I knew this would almost certainly mean that the other organisations linked to the NAVS would not join Animal Welfare Year. In this I was right. On the 11th April I received a letter from the Animals' Vigilantes advising that this organisation for young people would not be participating, and on the 5th May a similar letter was received from the Lord Dowding Fund for Humane Research. Later a refusal came from the International Association Against Painful Experiments on Animals.

When Animal Welfare Year's business brochure was published and we were forming up local support groups, I received a number of letters from members of the NAVS asking why their organisation was not participating to which I had to reply. In my answer I suggested that the writers take the matter up with NAVS headquarters. In the May/June, 1976 issue of their magazine *Animals' Defender*, the editor published the following statement:

The NAVS has received a number of inquiries asking if the Society is going to participate in Animal Welfare Year, a project involving a series of events arranged by an amalgamation of animal welfare societies whose aim is to draw attention to, and better the lives of, exploited animals.

While this Society wishes every success to the sponsors of this worthy cause it does not intend to join with these activities—for the following reasons. The stated aims of Animal Welfare Year are not unfortunately sufficiently radical for the NAVS to give them enthusiastic support. Also the interest focused on laboratory animals occupies only a part of the Animal Welfare Year programme.

The NAVS is totally engaged in its campaign to abolish experiments on live animals and therefore feels that it must dedicate its entire capabilities to this end and not diffuse its energies by linking them to other aspects of animal welfare which are already being well served by organisations devoted to other specific problems.

To be completely fair to the NAVS, with whom, as a sister anti-vivisection society, we enjoy the most cordial relations, I have published their statement in full. However this statement obviously did not satisfy many of the members and supporters of the NAVS, for in the September/October issue of the *Animals' Defender*, the Society published a full editorial on their non-participation. This was headed *NAVS and Animal Welfare Year—A Statement*, and reference was again made to the Year in the November/December issue of 1977.

Animal Welfare Year was primarily a national publicity campaign, designed to bring to the notice of the "vast silent majority" of the British Public what was being done to animals in their name, particularly since it is done legally under various Acts of Parliament and often with the money of taxpayers. As such, the campaign had to restrict itself to limited objectives and, as I stated earlier, the accent had to be on "realism" and not "idealism." Surely the whole point about such a campaign is that if the uncommitted can be made aware of the worst abuses of animals, whether they be animals used for research, animals farmed for food, pet animals or wild animals, this awareness, this interest in the minds of at least some of the uncommitted, will continue and grow as they become more involved. I certainly believe that this was the feeling of many of the supporters and branches of the NAVS and other organisations, since I cannot recall attending a single event during the whole of Animal Welfare Year anywhere in Britain where there was not a stand run by the local branch of the NAVS.

A similar response came from the Royal Society for the Protection of Birds, another organisation to refuse our invitation, despite a personal appeal from our President, Lord Houghton, to Lord Donaldson, President of the RSPB. The RSPB explained that it was the Society's policy only to become involved in an operation if it felt that it was able to devote time and expertise to the project. As the RSPB had been asked by the Nature Conservancy Council to become involved in the European Wetlands Campaign, their total resources would be directed towards that end and, for that reason, it was regretfully decided to decline the invitation to become involved in Animal Welfare Year. Once again there were few, if any, events I attended during the Year, where the RSPB were not in evidence.

A further example of this attitude was the PDSA. This organisation originally indicated support for Animal Welfare Year although it was not in a position to give a financial contribution. In August 1976, however, at the commencement of the Year proper, I was informed by Mr. E. C. L. Hulbert-Powell, Chairman of the PDSA, that the Society was concerned only with providing a free veterinary service for animals whose owners were unable to pay for private treatment and that the Society was unable to allow its objects to be confused with those of other participating societies whose activities, however laudable, might be clearly seen to be a matter of argument, if not controversy.

Of course, the NAVS was right in saying that the Year did not concentrate wholly on laboratory animals and did not go as far as the NAVS (or, for that matter, my own society) would wish in condemning vivisection, but we did succeed in focusing public attention on the whole subject of experimentation. In the case of the RSPB, they had a responsibility to publicise European Wetlands Year; but they could have used Animal Welfare Year for this purpose and given backing to their branches that did involve themselves in the Year. The PDSA's attitude on controversial issues is well known, but they too could have used the Year to publicise their own work and particularly Animal Welfare Year's concern for pet animals.

Wherever events for the Year were held, nearly all these organisations were represented—even though officially their societies were not participating—simply because the branches were not going to be left out of a local event which was providing publicity for the other animal welfare societies working in the area. Local branches of national organisations and indeed individual members want *action*, and Animal Welfare Year gave them the opportunity for such action.

In an interview with *Animal Welfare*, the journal of the BUAV, Miss Janet Fookes, M.P., now Chairman of the RSPCA Council was asked what she felt was the most important feature to have emerged from Animal Welfare Year. She replied that it was the phenomenon of so many animal welfare societies working together in concert. She thought it regrettable that not all the larger societies had participated, but there had been more than enough working together to prove that even this traditionally argumentative body of organisations could, when they chose, act in constructive harmony. [2]

I shall return to the vexed question of organisations working together and the problems which this entails, but for the moment I will say that whatever the problems, we have got to find a way to co-operate if we are going to achieve our aims. I believed that a way has been found and that is through the joint consultative bodies which, in my view, were the major success story of Animal Welfare Year. The approach of these bodies can be summed up in this paragraph taken from the introduction to a paper submitted to the Home Office Advisory Committee by one of the bodies, the Committee for the Reform of Animal Experimentation. This introduction stated:

Whilst some of us hold a declared position in favour of total prohibition of the use of living animals for some or even all experimental work, others, while equally moved and concerned about what is happening, take a less extreme view. *We joined together without prejudice to our wider aims*, to achieve the fullest range of improvements possible without immediate amending legislation from the Government.[3]

Illegal use of Gin Trap.
This young badger was found caught in a gin trap not far from London. This type of trap is illegal and the badger is also protected in law.
(Photograph by courtesy of "Surrey Mirror").

Not all birds enjoy legal protection.
(Photograph by the Author).

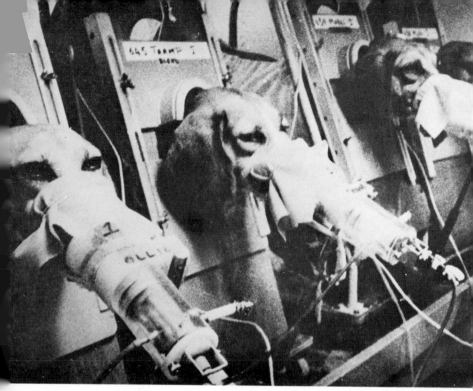

Smoking Beagles—the photograph which aroused the publics anger over animal experiments.

The Laboratory Animal—a simple injection experiment.
The substance injected may be innocuous but can also result in severe pain and suffering. *(Photograph by "Globe & Mail" Toronto).*

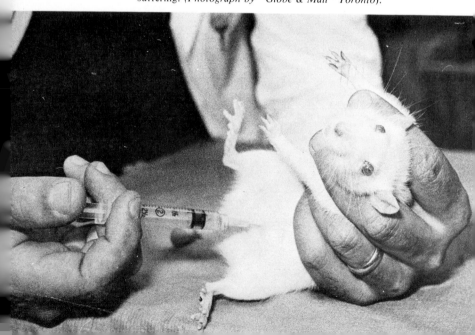

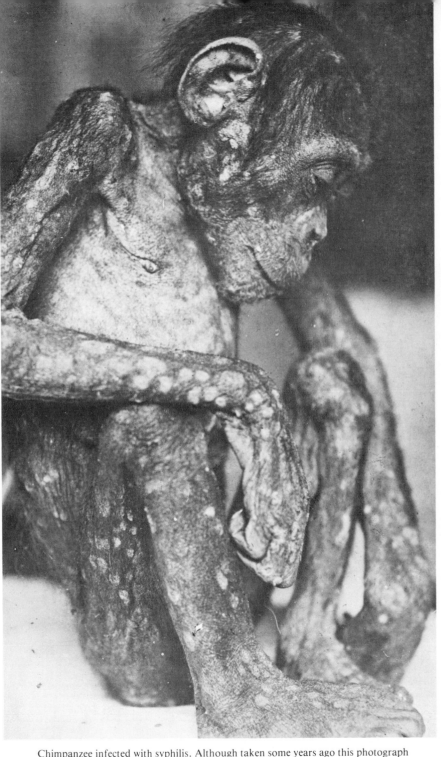

Chimpanzee infected with syphilis. Although taken some years ago this photograph from Denmark vividly illustrates what can be the result of a "simple injection"

The veal calf growing to market weight in a crate.
(By kind permission of Ruth Harrison).

The misery of close confinement of the breeding sow.
(By kind permission of Ruth Harrison).

The modern poultry packing station takes on the brave new world look with the slaughterman standing by to ensure that birds escaping the automated equipment are 'cut'.
(By kind permission of Ruth Harrison).

CHAPTER VII

The Run-Up to the Year and Near Disaster

Things were not going well. The Board was becoming increasingly concerned over finance and our meetings at the beginning of 1976 were taken up more and more with this subject. As I have said, my original costing for the Year had been fifty thousand pounds on the basis of employing a salaried organiser and working very much on a "shoe-string" budget. When we appointed the agency of Dexter, Brent and Paterson to handle the campaign though, we had widened our horizons considerably on the basis of the agency's confidence in securing funding from commercial organisations. Nearly two thousand letters were sent out to all the major commercial companies in Britain, as well as to a number of charitable trusts, but the response had been very poor. The final accounts for the Year record that donations from commercial sources and charitable trusts amounted to only £6,025, two thousand pounds of which was donated by one organisation, the J. Arthur Rank Group Charity.

It is difficult to find an explanation for this sad lack of response, particularly from the large and wealthy pet food manufacturers, but I think that there were a number of factors involved. The delay in publishing the business brochure, which was due to our efforts to gain royal patronage, was one reason, as was the fact that we did not obtain patronage. At that time, the country was facing a very difficult economic crisis, which obviously affected the charitable giving of many commercial organisations. I think too that perhaps some of our areas of concern, even though we kept away from the hunting issue, were "too near the knuckle" for some organisations. Finally, perhaps animal welfare is not, in the view of many, such an attractive field for charitable giving as other areas of human need.

Whatever the reasons for this lack of support, the fact remained that funding was becoming a big problem. Before this stage was reached, however, we had held a further delegates' conference on 4th December 1975. This was so that our plans for Animal Welfare

Year could be laid before the representatives of the participating societies. During the Conference, the agency presented an outline of the programme of events, illustrated with slides, also giving details of the areas of concern we hoped to tackle during the Year.

The programme of major events was very impressive and included such things as a film premiere, an art gallery exhibition and a special service at Westminster Abbey. I lost count of the number of meetings I attended or of the people Miss Jeannette Dexter of the agency and I visited to discuss the planning of events, to gain support for promotional schemes, or to ask for financial donations. The period from October 1975 to January 1976 was a hectic time for all of us, but in spite of all our efforts, the financial problem continued to worsen.

At meetings in January the agencies had agreed to reduce the termination clause in their contract from three months to one month, which provided the Board with a breathing space before the necessity arose of making a decision on whether we could afford to continue. The agencies had further agreed to reduce their scale of fees to assist the financial situation until such time as further funds became available. It should be borne in mind that both agencies were commercial profit-making organisations and it was therefore more than generous of them to suggest working at a loss.

Unfortunately, matters did not show any sign of improving and at the meeting of the Board in early March 1976 Miss Dexter recommended that unless there was a considerable improvement in income before the next meeting at the end of the month, the continued appointment of the agency should be seriously re-considered and a decision taken on the future of Animal Welfare Year.

There was no such improvement in our finances and at the meeting of 29th March 1976 it was resolved on Miss Dexter's recommendation that Dexter, Brent and Paterson be given one month's notice. This decision was reached with the greatest regret, as we deeply appreciated all the work they had done. Discussion followed as to the future. Did we abandon the whole idea of Animal Welfare Year, or did we try to continue in a somewhat lower key? I was determined that the Year should continue and should succeed, but a number of the directors felt that we should call it a day. I read out to the Board extracts from some of the letters I had received from members of animal societies and the public. The sentiments expressed in many of these letters were similar to one another. One supporter in Wales wrote:

> I see Animal Welfare Year as quite the best thing that has happened for the animals since the early part of the 19th century and I remain convinced that unless all the animal charities can be united in some way—the future is bleak for each one of them.

I ended my appeal to my fellow directors with the dramatic words:

> For the sake of all who are supporting us and for the sake of the animals, let us continue—and if we fail then at least let us fail gloriously.

I had one further card up my sleeve. When I had realised that whatever happened we were going to have to dispense with the services of the agency, I discussed the whole problem with my own directors in Edinburgh. I was therefore able to announce that the St. Andrew Animal Fund would inject a further ten thousand pounds into the campaign if at any stage this became necessary to keep the Year solvent. It had further been agreed that the whole campaign could be run from the offices of the Scottish Society for the Prevention of Vivisection in Edinburgh.

We therefore decided that Animal Welfare Year was to continue with the national headquarters in Edinburgh and the services of Infopress Limited should be retained to handle publicity. The consultancy also agreed to share with my office the planning of national Events. After removing all the files and materials for the Year from the London office of the agency to my office in Edinburgh, I was faced with an almost herculean task. Up until this time I had been Chairman of the Campaign—which was exacting enough, but now I was Chairman, organiser and chief bottle-washer all rolled into one. It was only when I was endeavouring to sort through the masses of files and papers on returning with them to Edinburgh that I began to realise the size of the task.

Fortunately, I secured the help of Miss Gennie Poole, who quickly became my right arm, and I was able to leave in her capable hands nearly all the administration of the Year as far as contact with the local groups was concerned.

During the course of the Year we received from time to time

complaints from groups and supporters that material or promotional goods they had ordered had not arrived on time for an event. Leaving aside the fact that frequently we received such orders only three or four days before an event, coupled with postage delays and industrial action, I often wondered whether the groups and supporters realised that apart from voluntary workers who helped out now and then the whole campaign was being run virtually by three people, (and I was away much of the time).

It had been decided that the official launch of the Year would be held at the Press Club in London on the 7th July 1976, which was a month or so before the actual commencement of the Year. This was done because we were anxious to achieve early publicity in order to encourage the public to become involved. We had also secured a preview night at Drury Lane on 17th July for the American smash-hit musical *A Chorus Line*. The launch was held as planned with a good turn-out from the press, oddly enough including a German film crew who filmed the whole of the opening speeches for a programme they were preparing. I never found out if the programme was screened to German television viewers or, if it was, what they thought about Animal Welfare Year.

In view of our financial situation, I decided to approach the RSPCA for a further grant to support the Year. I attended the full meeting of the Council in July and, as a result of my pleading and in the face of certain opposition, the RSPCA made a further grant of five thousand pounds, bringing their total contribution to ten thousand pounds.

During this period, a number of the directors resigned from the Board. The first was Mrs D. Hegarty of FRAME, who in December 1975 resigned owing to pressure of work. In February, David Whiting of Beauty Without Cruelty resigned due to an overseas tour and was replaced as director by Princess Anne Galitzine, a council member of BWC. In May, Peter Roberts of Compassion in World Farming resigned, also because of work pressures and July saw the loss of Arthur Parratt of the Cats' Protection League, who had left his job as Secretary of the League. Colin Platt of ISPA also resigned at this time as he was going overseas.

Directors appointed to fill these vacancies were, in addition to Princess Galitzine, Harold Bywater, (ISPA), Lady Alison Follett

(Barnes Wildlife and Animal Welfare Group), Sidney Hicks (BUAV), and Stanley Osborn (CPL), all of whom were appointed in July, 1976.

At this time I was coming in for a great deal of criticism, both at board meetings and outside the boardroom, for being autocratic (which, incidentally, I freely admit to), for taking decisions without prior agreement, for exceeding my authority as Chairman, and generally for riding rough-shod over all and sundry. I think some of the criticism was justified, but those who were my critics were not working under the strain of being Chairman of the campaign. It may be a board of directors which takes decisions, but at the end of the day it is the Chairman who has to shoulder the responsibility for success or failure. In addition, it has to be appreciated that there were many decisions which had to be taken immediately—and I took them.

Apart from all these valid arguments, I knew the direction I wanted to take to make the Year a success and, come hell or high water, I was going to take it. During this rather difficult time most of the directors gave me welcome support, but I think only one of my fellow directors really understood all my problems. When I learnt of her sudden death in December 1977, I knew I had lost a very good and very dear friend in Anne Galitzine.

In August 1976, Colonel Roosmalecocq, Secretary of the National Canine Defence League, resigned, since, as he explained in his letter, he had just too many commitments. I was very sorry to receive Alexander's letter, since I had great respect for his advice and clear thinking at board meetings. In November, Mrs Glenda Spooner of Ponies of Britain also resigned, as she was unhappy about the differences of opinion which had been developing for some time between Mr. Freddie Burden and myself. She was also concerned at the amount of money which was being spent with, in her view, little result. These vacancies were filled by Alan Whittaker of the BUAV, appointed in November 1976 (Sidney Hicks who had retired as Secretary of the BUAV subsequently represented the Animal Welfare Trust), and Derek Hanchett-Stamford of the Performing Animals' Defence League, who was appointed in December 1976.

Despite all the difficulties and problems Animal Welfare Year was now well established and the public were responding

57

magnificently to the challenge presented by the campaign. In all, sixty-three local co-ordinating groups gave their support to the Year. Some of these groups were branches of national societies, others were local societies or sanctuaries, yet others were amalgams of local societies and branches. Many others, however, were formed by enthusiastic members of the public in order to give their support to the Year. In addition, many thousands of individuals assisted in one way or another.

To help with fund-raising, Animal Welfare Year produced a range of promotional goods featuring the logo—badges, car stickers, adhesive labels, T-Shirts and notelets. Of all these goods, the notelets were the most successful. Produced from original drawings gifted to the Year by the Isle of Mull artist Mrs Elizabeth Shields, eighty thousand notelets were printed and packed for sale in plastic containers containing eight notelets and envelopes. It was planned to publish a small mail order catalogue for selling promotional goods on a large scale. An independent company retained to handle the merchandising for the Year, however, failed to honour its agreement to produce the catalogue, which resulted in considerable loss of income to the Year and difficulties in providing local groups with goods for sale at events.

Activities of the local co-ordinating groups varied considerably and the events were diverse and imaginative. These included sponsored walks, swims, silences, fasts, cycle tours and pony rides. There were also parties and processions, stage shows and dances, Animal Welfare Year produced twenty thousand business brochures, ten thousand crown and two thousand double-crown posters, sixty thousand general enquiry leaflets and forty thousand copies of information leaflets. In addition, nine news letters were published at roughly six weekly intervals to keep everyone informed of what was happening.

Although the local co-ordinating groups and many of the participating societies gave magnificent support to the Year, a number of the societies seemed to take the view that having lent their name to the Year as a participating organisation this was the end of their obligations. These societies failed to appreciate the opportunity created by Animal Welfare Year for publicising their own work to a greater extent than would be possible in normal circumstances. Some of the societies I visited were not even displaying Animal Welfare Year posters in their premises and held no stocks of the Year's promotional goods to sell to their members—at a profit to themselves.

As a footnote to this chapter on the organisation of the Year, I might return briefly to the subject of unity to illustrate how fragmentation and disunity affects others. Animal Welfare Year lost two opportunities for promotion schemes with pet food manufacturers for this reason. Pedigree Petfoods turned down our invitation to participate in a promotion due to the economic situation and also because they did not wish to be dragged in, however innocently, to any inter-society squabbles and differences of opinion. With a large number of participating organisations they believed such differences were bound to arise, however tactfully the programme was controlled by the central organisation. Spillers Foods were just as direct since they were not convinced that the amalgam of animal welfare societies would remain in accord throughout the preliminary and on-going periods. As the aims and objectives of the individual societies varied quite considerably problems might arise at the most inappropriate time.

We proved them wrong during Animal Welfare Year. We did work together although at times the going was rough.

CHAPTER VIII

National & Major Local Events of the Year

The first national event of the Year was a preview of *A Chorus Line* at Drury Lane on the evening of 17th July 1976. We were extremely fortunate to obtain this prestige event through the good offices of our agency. *A Chorus Line*, conceived, choreographed and directed by Michael Bennett, won nine Tony Awards, and was the first musical for nearly twenty years to win the Pulitzer Theatre Prize. In the United States, the *New York Times* devoted four columns to a "rave" review, while *Newsweek* devoted a front cover to "Broadway's New Kick." When the show came to London, the *Sunday Times* colour supplement published a four page review of the show's success in the States and Canada. Unfortunately, when it comes to a preview, the critics and theatre-going public have not seen the show, something which makes selling seats somewhat difficult. Once *A Chorus Line* had opened in London, it became a "hit" and tickets were scarcer than gold-dust.

When a charity takes a preview night, the production costs and the theatre have to be paid for, and the profit therefore is not nearly as good as many people who have paid for expensive seats might imagine. Our income on this show, including money earned from the sale of tickets, advertising revenue from the souvenir programme and donations, amounted to £7,751; the expenditure, including the cost of the production, commission on ticket sales, advertising, printing and postage totalled £7,283. Our profit on the venture was therefore less than five hundred pounds, small reward for an enormous amount of effort on the part of many people involved. Nevertheless, it was a magnificent evening and a good publicity boost for the Year, since the preview was well covered, particularly on radio, where there were five interviews on LBC, an hour long *Phone-In* on *Capital*, and a mention on Radio One. The souvenir programme contained a list of all the participating societies, an introduction by the Chairman, and details of the four areas of concern.

The official opening of the Year in August was marked at Westminster Cathedral, where on the first of the month, Canon Bartlett, the Administrator of the Cathedral, preached on Animal Welfare Year. At evensong at St. Pauls Cathedral, Canon Webster gave an address on Animal Welfare Year and the work of the animal societies. From the beginning of August that year until early October, when the Feast of St. Francis of Assisi marks World Day of Prayer for Animals, special services were to be held in churches and cathedrals up and down the country.

It was at evensong at Westminster Abbey on Sunday 3rd October 1976 that the Year first started happening for me. After all the preparation, after all the hard work and worry, the Year at long last came alive. A special order of service was printed featuring the Animal Welfare Year logo and the arms of the Abbey. David Jacobs read one of the lessons and the sermon was preached by Hugh Montefiore, the then Bishop of Kingston and now Bishop of Birmingham. The normal congregation of some three hundred attending evensong in October was swollen to well over one thousand, and those who attended were privileged to take part in a most beautiful and moving service.

Hugh Montefiore opened his Address with the words:

Few of us in the Abbey this afternoon know one another. We are a great gathering of the unknown. But we have one great cause in common—animal welfare. What is more, we are convinced that this great common cause—animal welfare has something to do with God, or we would not have entered His house to worship. . . .

. . . .First, let us remind ourselves, if we need to do so, that the whole world is God's world. "Let everything that has breath" said the Psalmist, "let *everything* that has breath, praise the Lord."

The Bishop continued by stating his own position regarding animal welfare and protection by saying:

I simply take my stand on one unassailable point: no human being has the right to inflict unnecessary pain, fear, or stress upon any other living creature. To inflict such pain is bad for the person who inflicts it. To inflict such pain is bad for the animal which suffers from it. It is immoral and wrong, and it denies both the dignity of man and the dignity of animal creation.[1]

On 16th October, the Liverpool Young Vegetarians organised a full day event at the Catholic Chaplaincy Centre in Liverpool. "Food for Thought" was the first major event I attended outside London, and credit must go to the organisers, as it must to the local organisers of the other events I attended around Britain, for undertaking a mammoth task of putting together an exhibition, speakers, personalities, publicity and, very often, supplies of food.

A similar event at which Richard D. Ryder, then Chairman of the RSPCA Council and I both spoke was "The Alternative Way," held in October in Cheltenham. This event which was a great success on what must have been one of the wettest nights of the year, was organised by a group known as POLG (Protect our Livestock Group). The other speakers at this event were Mr Charles Irvine, the local Member of Parliament and Miss Damaris Hayman, the television comedienne. This was my first meeting with Damaris, and we have become very good friends since that meeting. She has now become the Secretary of the Farm Animal Welfare Co-Ordinating Executive (FAWCE).

On 2nd November, I spoke at an event at Gorebridge in Midlothian which featured a Fashion Show staged by Beauty Without Cruelty and compered by Betty Herring, Edinburgh Secretary of BWC, and with a guest appearance of the well-known television actor John Cairney. There were many other such events. There was one at Ashford in Kent, for example, where the speakers were Richard Ryder, John Aspinall of Howletts Zoo Park and Port Lympne Wildlife Sanctuary, and myself. Incidentally, I have always considered my views on animal welfare to be extremist, but John Aspinall referred to me as "a moderate"—and anyone who has heard John speak on this question will understand why!

The busiest months for these events were May and June 1977. On 4th May, I was speaking in the crypt of St. Margaret's Church at Lee in London; on 19th May in Glasgow; and on the 28th at the "Animal S.O.S." in Derby, where once again the speakers were Richard Ryder and myself, together with Phillip Whitehead, M.P. We were all together again on the 11th June at a "Brains Trust" in Guildford, where the other speakers were the television personality and animal man, Johnny Morris, Dr Gordon Latto, and Mr David Paterson. Richard Ryder and I shared so many platforms at that time in fact that we started referring to ourselves as "that well-known double act."

Apart from the serious events, there were many in lighter vein; a Gala Folk Night in Edinburgh organised by my assistant Gennie Poole, a musical evening in Cleveleys in Lancashire with singer Oliver Dewhurst, and Open Day at Chilham Castle (the home of one of the Year's Vice-Presidents, Viscount Massereene and Ferrard), a Silver Jubilee Fair at Barnes, a production at the Edinburgh "Fringe" Festival—*The Last of the Barnstormers*, staged by my wife, to mention just a few.

One of the most spectacular of all such events was the RSPCA Silver Jubilee and Animal Welfare Year Gala Silver Ball, held at the Lakeside Country Club, Frimley Green and organised by Chobham RSPCA. This magnificent Ball was largely the work of Commander and Mrs Innes Hamilton, and was attended by the President of Friends of Chobham, Miss Beryl Reid, and the actor Patrick McNee (Steed of the television *Avenger* series). Patrick McNee turned up again at another event, a coffee morning at Wallingford Town Hall in Oxfordshire, which raised over three hundred pounds for the Year. In a sense he really did "turn-up," as at the time he was filming in France and made a dash to Wallingford by jet, helicopter and car to arrive in time to honour his promise to the organiser, Mrs Joan Latto, that he would attend.

Mr Jeffrey Sion, Director of the Seen Gallery in London, held an exhibition of animal paintings at the Gallery in January 1977, and he most generously donated a percentage of the sales to Animal Welfare Year. This amounted to a cheque for over three hundred and fifty pounds. There were over one hundred paintings on exhibition and our President, Lord Houghton, purchased a painting of a fox cub when he and I attended the preview of the exhibition.

A national photographic competition was run for the Year in the *Amateur Photographer* magazine. There was a tremendous response and, as one of the judges, I had great difficulty in making a final selection from the variety of subjects submitted. Animal Welfare Year was grateful to the *Amateur Photographer* and the commercial companies which donated the prizes for this competition which were presented to the winners at the final Animal Welfare Year Conference on 14th December 1977.

One of the great disappointments of the Year was the special stamp issue. We made application to the Post Office for a special issue to mark Animal Welfare Year and were extremely fortunate in being selected from the thousands of applications for one of the six special issues in any one year—of which one is the Christmas issue. The Post Office indicated that the issue of six native wild animal stamps would be in February 1977, but later, and without further reference to Animal Welfare Year, it suddenly announced that the British Wild Animal series would be issued in October. Despite representations made at the very highest level, the Post Office would not change the issue date even though it was pointed out that the proposed date was two months after the end of Animal Welfare Year. The issue, which I think many would agree was one of the most attractive special issues in recent years, came out in October, but as the Year had ended, we were unable to reap any financial benefit through the sale of first-day covers.

Of all the events we organised, I think one of the most exciting was "Project Youth." This scheme was devised to involve young people in the Year and it received wide publicity in such magazines as *Scouting* and through the assistance of the Inner London Education Authority in particular. The Animal Welfare Year local co-ordinating groups also assisted in publicising the scheme in which schools, youth groups and individual children were asked to undertake a project for Animal Welfare Year. The project could be anything which related to animals, practical conservation, a study of a species or form of exploitation, or a fund-raising project. Another youth project was devised by the RSPCA which ran a national poster painting competition on the theme of Animal Welfare Year for members in their junior magazine *Animal Ways*.

Perhaps the Event which stands out most in my mind, however, was the two performances of Benjamin Britten's *Noyes Fludde* (the Chester Miracle play set to music), in Westminster Cathedral on 6th and 7th May, 1977. A review in the *Listener* caught the atmosphere of this production:

There was something ghostly and mysterious in the modern sense of these words, about the interior of Westminster Cathedral, as the 'animals' emerged from the shadowy aisles to enter Noye's ark. They were of course small children wearing animal masks; and the chirpy 'Kyrie Eleison' they were singing, I think was the same 'Kyrie' as the one sung by the sinister choirboys at the opening of the film, Lord of the Flies. But it is, obviously, improper to impose ghost-story fantasies on Noyes Fludde—this beautiful work, linking Covent Garden soloists with childrens' voices and with the hymns of an untrained congregation, made strange and dashing by the curious harmonies and triumphant bugles. [2]

The final event of the Year, which in fact was organised by the RSPCA, was a two day symposium on "Animal Rights" held at Trinity College, Cambridge, on 18th and 19th August 1977. The proceedings of the symposium have now been published, [3] and in his preface to the book the philosopher, Peter Singer, refers to the significance of the published papers presented at the symposium:

> Do not expect to find unanimity. The different perspectives in these papers testify to the coming together of diverse groups and individuals from many countries and different professions, all concerned with rights for animals. We cannot predict the future, but it is not impossible that when, a century hence, people ask where the newly victorious animal rights movement got started, historians will point to the meeting held at Trinity College in 1977. If like me, you were unable to be there, all you can do is kick youself and be thankful that, with the publication of this volume you can share in the ideas then presented.

Due to the necessity of husbanding our resources and indeed the lack of available funds with which to stage events, we had to cancel tentative plans for a number of the major events originally proposed by the agency. However, we did succeed in bringing Animal Welfare Year to the notice of a very large number of people throughout Great Britain as a result of these events and through them we also obtained very wide publicity for the Year in the press, on radio, and on television.

CHAPTER IX

Publicity

Although Animal Welfare Year did not officially begin until August 1976, a number of newspapers, including some influential provincial ones reported on the campaign as a result of a press release we put out at the end of 1975. This was valuable publicity, since we immediately began receiving letters of support from the public, frequently accompanied by donations.

The *Yorkshire Evening Press*, in a half-page article headed *Animal-Lovers Plan their Big Push,* described the Year as: "The biggest, the most ambitious animal charity spectacular that Britain has ever seen." The first "in depth" article, however, appeared in a national newspaper in June 1976, when the Sunday *Observer* colour supplement published a six-page report by Ena Kendall on the subject of animal experimentation. This was a well reasoned article presenting both sides of the argument and while accepting that vast improvements in human and animal health had been achieved through the use of experimental animals, the report emphasised:

> Scientists who actually do animal experiments are among those who say the Act's centenary, coupled with the launching this summer by 60 animal welfare societies of Animal Welfare Year, is an apt time to redefine our legislation on this contentious subject.

Miss Kendall quoted comments from a number of scientists working with animals. One senior scientist, for example, working at a cancer research institute told her:

> I object to working under a system that is supposed to authenticate me as a humane experimenter under cover of an Act that is totally inadequate and disregarded in this building. I don't like the deception of the public it involves.

67

The report also quoted comments from a senior animal technician, who together with two of her junior colleagues subsequently lost their jobs. In an interview with the press, the director of their laboratory stated: "It's true that these girls have been dismissed—two of them because of incidents involving memos and the third because she has been a troublemaker over a long period."[1]

Although he did not know it, the action of this research director was a stroke of good fortune for the animal welfare movement, since the senior laboratory technician was Miss Angela Walder, who has become a vigorous and outspoken opponent of animal experimentation. Although not a totally committeed anti-vivisectionist, Angela is in my opinion a most valuable asset to the movement because of her specialised knowledge and long experience of working in laboratories using animals.

At the official launch of Animal Welfare Year at the Press Club in London on 7th July 1976, Infopress, our consultancy, issued a "press kit" containing an introduction and a series of seven papers on the different areas of concern for the Year. This kit was sent out to the press and resulted, over the following months, in many detailed reports on the campaign and articles on one or other of the areas of concern. The next press release issued on behalf of the Year came in August 1976 on the actual centenary of the *Cruelty to Animals Act*. It was timed for the commencement of the Year and appropriately dealt with the memorandum on animal experiments submitted to the Home Secretary by a group under the chairmanship of Lord Houghton. In due course this document was to become known as the "Houghton/Platt" Memorandum.

Nearly every national and provincial newspaper gave space to this report and generally welcomed this new approach. In an editorial on the subject the *New Scientist* praised the memorandum in enthusiastic terms:

Backed by Lord Platt, Lord Houghton, the Chairman of Animal Welfare Year and by members of the RSPCA and the Animal Welfare Parliamentary Group, the document is well reasoned. It details enough areas of disquiet to establish the need for reform. The document is unhysterical and, indeed, it emphasises the clash between "the public interest in suppressing or controlling cruelty to, and the abuse of, animals, and the public interest in medical research, safety of drugs and safeguards against the use or marketing of harmful substances.''

The editorial was also severely critical of the attitude of the Research Defence Society to the memorandum:

The Research Defence Society's response to the paper has been bitterly disappointing. . . . At a time when the other side is making such constructive moves in the 'vivisection' debate, the Research Defence Society should think again. [2]

Even that "establishment" journal of the medical profession, the *Lancet*, commented on the Houghton/Platt Memorandum and declared that the hundred year old Act was ripe for review. The *Lancet* pointed to two aspects of research where conditions have changed and therefore merited serious consideration:

The first is the object of the experiments. The number of them has increased hugely, to about five and a half million a year, and the object has changed in that most of them, three and a half million, are not done for medical research but by commercial concerns to test additives, detergents and substitutes for tobacco.

The other matter which required consideration was the constitution and functions of the Home Office Advisory Committee, the keystone of the Houghton/Platt Memorandum. Here the *Lancet* warned:

All change, even for the better, involves discomfort. The Establishment would hate the amended committee; experimenters would be upset; the extremists would still be dissatisfied. But the thoughtful public might feel happier that an improvement had been made. [3]

The publicity resulting from the Houghton/Platt Memorandum set the seal on coverage during the remainder of the Year. Apart from regular articles and reports in the national, provincial and local press, the supporters of the Year conducted a massive letter-writing campaign to editors which added considerably to the overall press coverage.

A number of unexpected magazines and journals reported on the Year, including a tongue-in-cheek article in *Punch* titled *Mad*

69

Englishmen and Dogs. Another magazine which published an eight inch single column report on the Year was *Jackie,* a magazine for teenage girls. I mention this report specially, not because of the column inches devoted to the Year, but the thought-provoking response; we received over one thousand letters from girl readers as a direct result.

Woman magazine published a three page article on the vivisection debate, *Need There be so Many Animal Experiments?,* and other newspapers and journals dealt with special areas of concern. The *Western Mail,* for example, carried a special investigation into the Welsh pony trade, *Slaughter of the Innocents*; the *Scotsman* a report on cosmetics and furs, *Beauty Without Animals*; the *Yorkshire Post, They Eat Horses, Don't They*; and the *Guardian* ran a special supplement on Animal Welfare Year and responsible pet ownership.

The support we received from radio and television was superb. I personally completed over ten hours air-time on radio and television in interviews, phone-ins, discussions and full length programmes. These programmes varied from an interview on the BBC television programme *Pebble Mill at One* to local radio shows. I travelled all over the country for general interest and magazine programmes, farming and religious spots, early morning and late evening shows.

At times the travelling involved for short interviews was immense. For an eight minute interview on HTV, I took the morning flight from Edinburgh to Birmingham, thence by train to Bristol and by taxi to the studio. I returned to Edinburgh on the night train from Bristol—a total of some thirteen hours travelling for an interview lasting only a few minutes. It seems disproportionate, but one has to remember the enormous audience watching television—even at an off-peak time. During that one interview I probably spoke to more people than by speaking to live audiences of say one hundred people every night of the year, for perhaps four or five years.

I think perhaps the worst journey during that period was for a two hour phone-in programme on Radio Plymouth. I travelled from Edinburgh to London on the night train, had breakfast in London, met Princess Galitzine, who was sharing the programme, and then caught the 9.30 train to Plymouth. We arrived at 1.20

p.m., took a taxi to the studio and went straight on the air at 2 p.m. There was a quick coffee with the presenter when the programme finished at 4 p.m., a taxi to the station to catch the 5 p.m. train to London, dinner, and then the night train back to Edinburgh. The total travelling time was about thirty hours, with a break of two hours on the air in the studio.

During the Year, a number of full length documentaries were screened on television. *The Guineapig and the Law*, shown in the BBC *Horizon* series, was one such programme and the BBC 2's *Current Account* was another. *Nationwide* gave coverage during the Year to a numbr of items relating to animal welfare, including cosmetic testing on animals, the trade in the transportation of horses for slaughter, and alternative humane methods of research.

The churches also gave publicity and support for the Year, not only in the form of special services, but also by drawing attention to the importance of Animal Welfare Year in other ways. The Church of Scotland at its General Assembly in May 1977, approved the following deliverance:

> Note that this is Animal Welfare Year and commend the welfare of domestic animals, farm animals, laboratory animals and wild animals to the consideration of all citizens; and urge that no experiments be carried out on living animals unless they are vitally necessary to human or animal welfare. [4]

The following year, after due consideration of the areas of concern raised during Animal Welfare Year, the Church and Nation Committee in its report to the General Assembly included a three page deliverance on animal welfare which was accepted and endorsed by the Assembly. (The deliverance is printed in full in appendix D, since I consider that in this statement the Church of Scotland has given a lead among Christian churches on this moral issue of our time).

A private motion came before the General Synod of the Church of England in November 1977 applauding the promotion of the Year. The motion welcomed the declared objective of the Year and urged members of the Church of England and others to have regard for this objective; to make more widely known the plight of many animals and birds; to take all possible steps to make life more tolerable for such creatures; to safeguard those species threatened

71

with extinction; and to prevent ignorance, neglect, cruelty, degradation and commercial exploitation of animals. The resolution was adopted with only one vote against. The Society of Friends in Scotland also adopted a resolution supporting the Animal Welfare Year Campaign.

Another feature of publicity for the Year was the large number of exhibitions mounted either by local groups or by independent organisations. One of the most successful of these was the "Man, Exploiter or Guardian" exhibition, organised by the Anglican Society for the Welfare of Animals and the Friends Animal Welfare and Anti-vivisection Society (now Quaker Concern for Animal Welfare) which travelled the country and in May 1977 was on display in the west cloister of Westminster Abbey.

Films were used extensively during the campaign. The RSPCA made all their films available, as did Compassion in World Farming, Ponies of Britain, the Cats Protection League and my own Society and Fund. Pedigree Petfoods Education Service also very kindly loaned us a number of prints of each of their three educational films.

Whatever else may be said about the Year, there can be no doubt that it generated more publicity for animals than they had had at any time in the past. In doing this, there can be little doubt that we drew the attention of the public and government to the urgent need for action.

CHAPTER X

Areas of Concern and the Joint Consultative Bodies

Without any doubt at all the major success of Animal Welfare Year lay in demonstrating that the animal welfare societies could work together in harmony and for a common purpose. This sense of unity prepared the ground for the formation of a number of joint consultative bodies as an effective means of continuing this new awareness of the power of collective action.

As mentioned, Animal Welfare Year was directly responsible for gaining maximum publicity for the Houghton/Platt Memorandum submitted to the Home Secretary in May 1976. Following an exploratory meeting with Dr Shirley Summerskill, the Minister of State at the Home Office, and her advisers, the group under the chairmanship of Lord Houghton, met the Home Secretary, Merlyn Rees, on 15th February 1977, when agreement was reached on the need to amend some aspects of the administration of the *Cruelty to Animals Act, 1876.*

As a result of the success of this meeting, the Houghton group decided that it was necessary to continue to press for further reforms in the use of animals for research. The group was therefore formalised as the Committee for the Reform of Animal Experimentation (CRAE). In addition to the original signatories to the Houghton/Platt Memorandum [1], representatives of the British Union for the Abolition of Vivisection and the National Anti-Vivisection Society were appointed in a private capacity to membership of CRAE. Membership of CRAE is personal and is not open to organisations.

The CRAE Committee established lines of communication with the Department of the Home Office responsible for animal experimentation and now holds regular meetings with senior members of the Department. The Committee also has access to the Home Secretary when there is need for consultation on important issues outside the range of responsibility of the Department. It is important, in my view, to note that no animal society prior to the formation of CRAE had been able to achieve regular contact with the Home Secretary or the Home Office at this level.

On 7th September 1977, CRAE submitted written evidence and later gave oral evidence to the Home Secretary's Advisory Committee's Enquiry on the L.D. 50 (Lethal Dose 50 per cent) test. [2] This enquiry had been set up following CRAE's first meeting with the Home Secretary. The Advisory Committee's report on this enquiry which has since been published, is a most disappointing document. [3] The report, which contained a surprising number of serious inaccuracies for an official report, recommended that the L.D. 50 test should be allowed to continue, in spite of the evidence (much of it from scientific bodies) that the L.D. 50 was unreliable and of little scientific value. It would appear that the Committee bowed to international pressure to maintain this ritualistic test as a standard of toxicity.

The report did, however, make a number of important recommendations namely, that:

1.   LD 50 tests should be allowed to continue but
     (a) those who prescribe them or carry them out should always bear in mind that for "safety evaluation" purposes a degree of precision which calls for the use of a large number of animals is not necessary.

     (b) wherever practicable a limit test should be used in preference to an LD 50.

2.   There should be a closer liaison between the Home Office and the various advisory or regulatory bodies, both in this country and the EEC, concerned with the framing of regulations applicable to the transport, storage, marketing and use of toxic substances.

3.   The possibility of a uniform code of laboratory practice in relation to toxicity testing generally should be considered.

4.   LD 50 tests should not be begun at a time which will not ensure adequate supervision of the animals during the expected period of maximum effect.

5.   By means of a condition attached to licences experiments on primates should be made subject to the same safeguards as those afforded by the Act to experiments on dogs, cats and equidae.

Apart from the actual recommendations, the report also made a number of interesting comments and observations on the use of living animals for research purposes and the responsibilities of those who use them:

a cruel experiment under the Act is one where the pain caused by it was not justified by any resultant benefit or that it had been improperly conducted—as, for example, by neglect of the 'pain' condition. (Paragraph 11).

the experimenter will degrade himself and the society of which he forms part if he gives no thought to the aggregate of pain he imposes on others for his own, human, ends even though the sufferer has no concept of the quantities involved. (Paragraph 12).

infliction of pain on an animal, then, amounts to cruelty when the pain is not compensated by the consequential good. (Paragraph 12).

the human good envisaged must be a serious and necessary good, not a frivolous or dispensable one, if the infliction of pain on animals is to be ethically acceptable. (Paragraph 12).

an animal may suffer severe pain—say at night—for a considerable period before it is killed. (Paragraph 13).

no test in which severe suffering could reasonably be foreseen should be started at a time when technicians and other staff could not be continuously available. (Paragraph 16 (b)).

the possibility of the issue of a uniform code of practice should be examined and also a code of conduct or ethics embracing a wider issue of the responsibility of all concerned in experiments on animals for the proper treatment of the animals in their charge. (Paragraph 16 (b)).

technicians, animal handlers, licensees and indeed any staff working in an experimental laboratory should—if they do not already—feel free to express an unease or misgiving about the welfare of animals under experiment to those responsible for the animals in question. If they feel that their view is ignored or dismissed too lightly they should contact personally, by telephone or letter, the Home Office Inspectorate. (Paragraph 16 (b)).

Under the chairmanship of Lord Houghton, CRAE will continue to present a concensus of animal welfare opinion to the government on the use of living animals for research.

At a conference held on 19th March 1977, the horse societies of Britain discussed the problems relating to the welfare and protection of horses and ponies and, as a result of the conference, the National Joint Equine Welfare Committee (NJEWC) was formed, representing these societies.

Animal Welfare Year was concerned over the expanding trade in horse-meat exported to EEC countries. In 1976 the trade more than trebled, and in the first four months of 1977, the trade again doubled compared with the same period the previous year.[4] It seems to be the general pattern at sales throughout the country that the majority of horses, ponies, mares in foal, and mares with foals are bought for slaughter. At one sale in 1978, more than two hundred out of the three hundred New Forest ponies and foals offered for sale went for slaughter.[5]

This trade is frequently the cause of cruelty, one of the major factors being that there are only five slaughter-houses in this country which have licences to export to Europe. This results in animals having to travel long distances from sale to slaughter-house. In March 1977, magistrates were told a story of "appalling carnage" when they heard a case concerning thirty-three horses and ponies which had travelled from Wales to Norfolk, a journey of twelve hours. Only one animal was on its feet on arrival: some had suffocated, others had to be immediately slaughtered and the remainder had bruises and cuts and were sweating. A fine of forty pounds was imposed.[6]

Another cause for concern was that transport regulations require that mares with foals have to be partitioned off separately. As a result, slaughterers or dealers buying mares with foals sell the foals to a child or anyone who will buy, or even leave them in the market. The mare is then loaded into the transport vehicle, heavy with milk, for slaughter. Animal Welfare Year was successful in gaining considerable publicity on this trade in national, provincial and local newpapers and also on the *Nationwide* television programme.

In April 1977, Animal Welfare Year wrote to those societies concerned with the welfare of farm animals, inviting them to attend a conference to discuss the welfare and protection of farm animals. We appreciated that societies concerned with food animals, in common with societies working in other areas of animal exploitation, had different viewpoints on some areas of concern, notably on methods of intensive husbandry. Nevertheless, Animal Welfare Year believed there were enough areas of total agreement to permit societies to work together for a common purpose, without compromising their own position.

The Food Animals Conference under the chairmanship of Robin Corbett, M.P., was very successful and resulted in the formation of the Farm Animal Welfare Co-ordinating Executive (FAWCE), with Mr Corbett as Chairman. This committee now represents fifteen societies and a number of independent members. Its terms of reference are to discuss, investigate, review and make recommendations relating to the improvement of conditions and the protection of animals, birds and fish used for the production of food or farmed for other purposes.

One of FAWCE's priorities has been to support the campaign to abolish the export of live food animals for slaughter or further fattening. On 24th November 1977, FAWCE, in conjunction with the RSPCA, held a successful mass lobby in the House of Commons on the live export issue. More recently, in September 1979, FAWCE submitted to the Minister of Agriculture, Fisheries and Food a Memorandum entitled *Pre-slaughter Stunning Methods and Slaughterhouse Operation in British Abattoirs*. This paper was the result of a painstaking study by FAWCE following the publication of three separate and quite independent expert reports, all of which cast doubt on the efficacy of our slaughterhouse procedures.[7] As one of these reports, *A Review of Pre-Slaughter*

Stunning in the E.C., stated, "in order to comply with the law a 'stunning appliance' must be used, whereas success—in the sense of actual stunning—often remains doubtful." As a result of this review, FAWCE has requested the Minister to set up a committee of enquiry to answer the questions raised in the memorandum and to make recommendations.

Animal Welfare Year gave qualified approval to the Department of the Environment's Working Party's report on dogs and welcomed the comments on the report made by the Joint Advisory Committee on Pets in Society (JACOPIS). JACOPIS was formed prior to Animal Welfare Year and in addition to the Pet Animal Welfare Societies, it also represents the Pet Food Manufacturers Association, the British Veterinary Association, the Kennel Club and local authorities.

The protection of wildlife presented so many varied and difficult problems that Animal Welfare Year agreed to concentrate on particular aspects in addition to the general campaign, to make the public aware of the importance of wildlife and wild places. One such area of concentration was in co-operation with the Mammal Society and Friends of the Earth in the National Otter Survey being undertaken to establish the present otter population of Great Britain. This survey was organised by Paul Chanin of the Department of Biological Sciences of the University of Exeter on behalf of the Mammal Society. Animal Welfare Year asked for volunteers to assist in the National Otter Survey and a large number of introductory letters, papers on the methods of conducting the survey, and survey details forms were sent out from Animal Welfare Year headquarters. Publicity was also given to the Friends of the Earth book on the otter, *The Declining Otter—A Guide to its Conservation* by Angela King, John Ottaway and Angela Potter.

Animal Welfare Year was also represented at the Joint Otter Group Conference organised by the Nature Conservancy Council in June 1977. As a result of this conference the Council approached the Minister of the Environment to grant protection to the otter and with effect from 1st January 1978, the otter was placed on the Schedule of Protected Animals in England and Wales (not in Scotland) under the *Conservation of Wild Creatures and Wild Plants Act, 1975.*

The second specific matter on which Animal Welfare Year endeavoured unsuccessfully to persuade the government to act was the permitted use of the cruel poison strychnine for the killing of moles. Regulations made under the *Animals (Cruel Poisons) Act, 1962* prohibits the use of strychnine for the killing of all animals with the one exception of moles. We pursued this matter with the Minister of Agriculture, Fisheries and Food and the Year also issued a press release on this question, which resulted in an article in the *New Scientist* (17th February 1977) by Professor Kenneth Mellanby.

There were many other issues connected with wildlife in which Animal Welfare Year endeavoured to play a part. We discussed with the Board of Trade the continued manufacture in Britain for export of the steel leghold trap (the "gin"), which was prohibited for use in England and Wales in 1958 and in Scotland in 1973. We also supported the campaign of Friends of the Earth to ban the importation of sperm oil and I presented a paper on this subject at a University Teach-In on Whales and Whaling held in Edinburgh in May 1977. This issue we took up in Parliament through two M.P.'s, Mr E Douglas Hoyle and Sir Bernard Braine.

Supporters of the Year took part in the demonstration outside Canada House in Trafalgar Square in London on 12th March 1977 against the annual slaughter of the harp seal. We also raised the issue of the use of dolphins and their transport around the world in cargo holds of planes for delivery to dolphinariums. On a number of occasions we became involved in the circus controversy. In particular, we criticised the proposal to include wild animal acts in the Billy Smart Royal Gala Big Top Show in the Home Park, Windsor, as part of the Silver Jubilee celebrations to be attended by the Queen.

Following a letter to the Queen's Private Secretary, Mr Derek Hanchett-Stamford, a Director both of the Year and of the Performing Animals Defence League, and I attended a meeting at Buckingham Palace with the Assistant Private Secretary. Unfortunately we were unable to persuade the Palace to have the programme altered, although we were assured that our original letter had been placed before Her Majesty, so at least the views of Animal Welfare Year and the many organisations and individuals who object to wild animal acts were made known to the Queen.

The RSPCA Education Department, in conjunction with the Royal Society for the Protection of Birds and Animal Welfare Year, organised an educational colloquium in November 1977. At this meeting all societies with an interest in education had the opportunity of discussing ideas on educational facilities offered by the societies. At the end of the day, there was general agreement that a more direct approach to schools and colleges was required, presented in an acceptable form for the use of teaching staff.

The Humane Education Council (HEC), under the chairmanship of David Paterson, now General Secretary of the British Union for the Abolition of Vivisection, was formed to achieve this objective. HEC now publishes the *Humane Education Journal* three times annually, to coincide with term times. This is a well produced journal containing informative articles and work projects for use by school staff.

At the suggestion of the Reverend Andrew Linzey, at that time a council member of the RSPCA, Animal Welfare Year organised a conference of all those animal welfare societies with specifically religious aims. It was hoped thereby to form a joint consultative body for the purpose of uniting Christians in the struggle to achieve justice for animals. Although the conference was held after the official end of the Year, we considered that the date was close enough for the conference to be held under the auspices of the Year. Dr Edward Carpenter, the Dean of Westminster chaired the conference and subsequently, agreed to be Chairman of the Christian Consultative Council for the Welfare of Animals which was formed as a result of the meeting.

In January 1980, the Christian Consultative Council published an excellent Report: "Vivisection—A Christian Approach" which will be circulated throughout the Christian community in Britain.

My one sorrow was that time did not permit us to attempt to bring together all those many organisations concerned in one way or another with the welfare and protection of wild animals. Admittedly, this is a most difficult area in which to try to obtain a concensus of opinion, since conservation interests and the anti-hunting campaigns seldom see eye to eye. I have made a number of attempts since the end of the Year to suggest to various organisations that a meeting should be arranged in the hope that a joint consultative body for wild animals could be established. I am still hopeful that such a body will be formed.

At the end of Animal Welfare Year, five joint consultative bodies, excluding JACOPIS, had been formed and now nearly three years later these bodies have become effective vehicles for contact with government departments, ministers, the press, schools, the churches and others on matters relating to the welfare and protection of animals.

The joint consultative bodies are the Christian Consultative Council for the Welfare of Animals, Committee for the Reform of Animal Experimentation (CRAE), Farm Animal Welfare Co-Ordinating Executive (FAWCE), Humane Education Council (HEC), National Joint Equine Welfare Committee (NJEWC).

CHAPTER XI

Not an End in Itself—But Rather a Beginning

Meetings of the Board of Directors of Animal Welfare Year continued at regular monthly intervals while the more public activities described in the preceding chapters were taking place. Apart from dealing with the areas of concern, the organisation of events, publicity, and with contact with societies and local groups, the Board also had to concern itself with financial and legal matters relating to the running of a limited company. This was particularly the case in the latter stages of the Year, as we had experienced enormous difficulties with a commercial company retained to assist with merchandising. This company had let us down badly through the actions of one of its employees and subsequently involved the Year in financial loss. Such problems, however are the lot of a board of directors and despite the difficulties, we were able to concentrate much of our time on the job in hand, that of making a success of Animal Welfare Year.

Unfortunately the opinions of Mr Burden and myself diverged and eventually Mr Burden resigned as a director. I had valued his advice at meetings and was conscious of the fact that he had been one of the prime movers in getting the Year started, but I was relieved to be able to accept his resignation since our clash of personalities was not helping the Year. The vacancy caused by Mr Burden's resignation was filled by Mr Peter Hunt of the Bransby Home of Rest for Horses.

Shortly after the commencement of the Year, I had received from a Mr Eric Hawtrey a very detailed and carefully thought out proposal for the setting up of a standing royal commission on animal welfare. The Board gave careful consideration to this document and after re-drafting, we put the proposal forward for legal drafting in a form suitable for introduction as a Private Member's Bill in Parliament.

The proposed commission, which would have included representatives from animal welfare organisations, would have undertaken a review of all existing legislation and regulations concerning domestic and wild animals and made recommendations for consolidating and updating the legislation. In the long term, the commission would have had responsibility for reviewing trends in the ways in which animals were exploited, in order that the animals used could be provided with safeguards. The commission would also have had the task of formulating and presenting to Parliament a code of animal protection covering the whole field of animal use and exploitation for whatever purpose. As it transpired events overtook our original intention to bring in a Private Member's Bill and the proposal for a standing royal commission on animal protection became one of the major planks in the later campaign to put animals into politics.

Another important question was that of the Universal Declaration of the Rights of Animals. Georges Heuse, Professor of Human Biology at the University of Paris, and the International League for Animals Rights were making great efforts internationally at this time to establish a Universal Declaration of the Rights of Animals. Meetings to discuss the draft of the Declaration had been held in Paris and Geneva and a final drafting meeting was held in London in September 1977. John Alexander-Sinclair, a director of the Year, had attended the Geneva meetings, and he and I both attended the London meeting to assist in the final drafting of the Declaration.

At a ceremony in Paris the International League for Animal Rights presented English and French texts of the Universal Declaration of the Rights of Animals to the Director General of UNESCO, together with the request that the Declaration be debated at the next UNESCO General Assembly in 1980. (For the full text of the Declaration, see Appendix E). During the ceremony,which was witnessed by seven hundred people, a message from Mr Morarji Desai, then Prime Minister of India and first Lord Chancellor of the Order of Nature, an order founded by the International League for Animal Rights, was read by the Indian Ambassador to France. In his message, Mr Desai spoke of the animal kingdom:

> Nature, civilisation and scientific instruments have combined gradually to wage a continuous but destructive war against the animal kingdom. At first there was a struggle for existence

between man and beast which man gradually won in his favour. Then animals suffered as a result of ravages on environment by man in the pursuit of his own pleasure or business. Even when domesticated and despite societies for the protection of animals, the animals have seldom had their due. [1]

The Declaration of the Rights of Animals is probably some two hundred years ahead of its time, nevertheless it sets out to establish principles to which man can aspire.

At the end of the Year, the Board published a campaign report which was sent out to all participating societies and local co-ordinating groups. We also issued a press release which resulted in a further spate of reports and articles in the press. Finally, on 14th December 1977, a final Animal Welfare Year conference was held at the Royal Commonwealth Society in London at which delegates from societies and groups were able to discuss and put forward their own views on the Year.

Long before the Year ended, Lord Houghton, Richard Ryder and myself had been discussing the next step which would follow the end of Animal Welfare Year. We did not want to lose the impetus and momentum we had achieved; indeed, we wanted to build on it. Lord Houghton was firmly of the view that what was needed was a political campaign. He referred to this in his speech at the Trinity College, Cambridge, Symposium on Animal Rights:

> My message is that animal welfare, in the general and in the particular, is largely a matter for the law. This means that to Parliament we must go. Sooner or later that is where we will have to go. That is where laws are made and where penalties for disobedience and the measures for enforcement are laid down.
>
> There is no complete substitute for the law. Public opinion, though invaluable and indeed essential, is not the law. Public opinion is what makes laws possible and observance widely acceptable. [2]

Lord Houghton returned to this idea in his speech at the final Animal Welfare Year conference, where there was general approval for his plan to "Put Animals Into Politics."

The publicity generated during the Year was almost entirely the work of Mrs Pat Chapman of Infopress. I had worked very closely with Pat during the campaign and had come to have a high regard for her expertise and her knowledge of animal welfare matters, which she had acquired during the Year. I was therefore very pleased when a number of societies[3] agreed to subscribe to a new company, to be known as Animal Advocates Information Service Limited, which was to be formed for the purpose of furthering the work of the animal welfare societies by a continuation of the publicity campaign started during the Year.

Although the Year had ended, it took a considerable time to wind up the affairs of the limited company. We were not able to hold our final annual meeting until 21st May 1979, when by special resolution of the annual meeting, the company was wound up. One of the reasons for delay was that in our policy statement of 28th March 1975, the Steering Committee had agreed that any funds remaining at the end of the Year would be repaid to participating societies *pro rata* to the amount of their original contribution. However, the balance remaining was so small that the refund only amounted to a little over three pence for every pound contributed.

The Board proposed therefore to offer societies an alternative and more effective way of using the funds remaining. We proposed that, if the societies agreed, we should hand over the balance to the Otter Haven Project of the Fauna Preservation Society and the Vincent Wildlife Trust, since we believed that efforts to save the endangered otter in England and Wales would have general appeal and approval. Before proceeding, however, we had to write to each organisation and obtain their written approval to pay over their share to the Trust. The majority of societies agreed to the Board's proposal and at the end of the day, we were able to give £1,041 to the Otter Haven Trust.

And so Animal Welfare Year ended. The *Spectator* said of the Year:

Animal Welfare Year has just ended and with it a brave and on the whole successful attempt to bring together the most fissiparous body of individuals this side of a school of amoebae. . .

. . .Dull it wasn't, as the ad says, and scratchy it could have been, but the Year coincided with, probably contributed to, the profound reappraisal the animal welfare movement is currently undergoing.[4]

Of course, there were many problems during the Year, not least of which was trying to keep the societies working together. But in this, we achieved far more than other "years." A report in the *Sunday Telegraph* on Age Action Year revealed some of their problems: "Bad planning, friction between charities who were supposed to pull together, poor publicity and the general economic climate are all being blamed." [5]

I believe that in Animal Welfare Year we achieved a great deal; we laid the framework for the future. One year, however, is a very short time in which to make any real impact on the entrenched positions of those with a vested interest in exploiting animals and who have the financial resources to maintain a powerful lobby in Parliament. Perhaps the dream of those who saw Animal Welfare Year as a beginning will become a reality, if historians record this century as being the time when man first accepted his place in the natural order, not as master but as a partner with all living things.

Animal Welfare Year was not an end in itself, but rather a beginning.

PART THREE

PUTTING ANIMALS INTO POLITICS

CHAPTER XII

General Election Co-ordinating Committee for Animal Protection

Early in 1978, Lord Houghton, Richard Ryder and I discussed the planning for our campaign to put animals into politics. A memorandum was drawn up as a discussion document for the animal welfare organisations to consider. In his introduction to this document Lord Houghton said:

> A general election during this year is a distinct possibility. It could come sooner or later than many expect. Much will depend upon events which have yet to unfold.

> Whenever the general election may come we should be prepared to grasp the opportunity to further the cause of animal protection: I call it "putting animals into politics." What I mean by that is obviously *not* party politics, but certainly to bring animal welfare within the policies of the political parties and therefore into the realm of *government responsibility*.

In due course, the document was sent to the chairmen and secretaries of the joint consultative bodies. The response to the memorandum was encouraging and we sent out more detailed proposals in April, inviting representatives of the joint bodies to attend a conference to discuss the proposal and the formation of a committee to organise a campaign.

The conference was held at the Royal Commonwealth Society in London with Lord Houghton in the chair. The delegates discussed the detailed proposals laid before them, including a draft of the letter to be addressed to the political parties, the full text of which appears in Appendix F. Agreement was reached on the approach to the parties and it was formally resolved to form a General Election Co-ordinating Committee for Animal Protection. Lord Houghton was elected as Chairman of the Committee, myself as Secretary and Prince Alexander Galitzine as Treasurer. It was also agreed that the campaign should be run from the offices of the Scottish Society for the Prevention of Vivisection in Edinburgh and that to cover initial financing, the joint consultative bodies be asked to contribute to the campaign fund. The five joint bodies formed during Animal Welfare Year, together with JACOPIS and the League Against Cruel Sports [1] were each requested to nominate two representatives to serve on the campaign committee.

The main problem facing the General Election Co-ordinating Committee for Animal Protection (GECCAP) was that like the rest of the country we did not know when the general election would take place. At that time the autumn of 1978 was a distinct possibility, but nobody except possibly the Prime Minister himself could do more than guess. This uncertainty made advance planning very difficult.

Our first task was to send out our letter to the political parties. This was duly done and by the date of the first meeting of GECCAP, we were able to announce that we had received acknowledgements of our letter from all five parties holding seats in Parliament, but excluding the Northern Ireland parties, whom we did not approach. We had also received confirmation of support for the campaign from the five joint bodies and the League Against Cruel Sports. In view of the progress made, Lord Houghton considered that we should now seek publicity for the proposals we had put to the political parties. Animal Advocates Information Service Limited therefore issued a press release on 3rd July 1978 which we headed *A Determined Call for Political Action on Animal Welfare*. A number of newspapers took up the story.

At this time the result of an opinion poll conducted by NOP Market Research on behalf of the League Against Cruel Sports produced some interesting findings on the public's reaction to blood sports. This poll revealed that 77% of the respondents were opposed to hare coursing; 74% were opposed to stag hunting; 72% were opposed to otter hunting and 60% were opposed to fox hunting. 58% were totally opposed to all hunting, while only 15% were actively in favour of hunting.

It has been frequently stated by the protagonists of hunting that the anti-hunting brigade are ignorant "townies" or socialist "lefties," but this poll showed that in rural areas 53% of the respondents were opposed to all forms of hunting, and of those who indicated that they supported the Conservative Party, 33% would not be in favour of laws to stop fox-hunting, but 41% would favour such a law. One of the most interesting findings from our point of view was that 9% of the respondents of voting age and 19% of those under eighteen years stated that a commitment on blood sports by a political party at the election would make them more inclined to vote for that party. [2]

The campaign to put animals into politics attracted criticism from certain sources because of the involvement of the League Against Cruel Sports in the campaign. Whatever the wisdom of involving the LACS and the blood sports issue in the campaign, there is no doubt in my mind that without the support of the League, the campaign would never have got off the ground. A national campaign of this kind requires considerable financing and in September, the Council of the League voted a contribution of twenty thousand pounds to GECCAP. This generous contribution was followed by ten thousand pounds each from the National Anti-Vivisection Society and the Scottish Society for the Prevention of Vivisection. Other societies followed suit, including a donation of eleven thousand dollars from the American International Fund for Animal Welfare and amounts ranging from a few pounds to one thousand pounds from other organisations. With the funds now available, we were able to print the campaign brochure, leaflets, posters and car stickers and start thinking in terms of press advertising.

The League's action at this time was of the utmost importance, since we were entering the month of the political party conferences and it was obviously essential for GECCAP to have a presence at each of the major conferences. In addition to the direct contribution to GECCAP, the League had also set aside a further ten thousand pounds to support the campaign and made available to GECCAP the services of one of their council members, Mr. Richard Course. It was agreed that Mr Course should organise the information centres and fringe meetings at the conferences.

As our campaign material became more widely available, we began to have trouble with "backsliders" among some of the member societies of the joint bodies. In the early days of the campaign JACOPIS had advised us that the majority of their member organisations did not wish to be associated with "Putting Animals Into Politics." The Universities Federation for Animal Welfare (UFAW) resigned membership of the National Joint

Equine Welfare Committee due to that Committee's participation in the political campaign.

Later, the Humane Education Council also withdrew due to the attitude adopted by the British Veterinary Association, the British Horse Society and the Royal Society for the Protection of Birds.

The RSPB advised the Humane Education Council that their association with the Putting Animals Into Politics brochure through membership of the Humane Education Council was causing grave concern since despite the disclaimer in the note on the inside front cover, it appeared to link the RSPB with standpoints expressly prohibited under the terms of their Royal Charter. The Royal Charter granted to the RSPB states as one of the objectives of the Society:

> To discourage the wanton destruction of any bird not killed for the purpose of food, *but to take no part in the question of killing game birds and legitimate sport of that character.*

Sad as that objective might be in the eyes of many, it did not conflict in my view with our campaign, which was concerned only with the hunting of otters, stags, hares and foxes with hounds.

As can be imagined, the pro-hunting press had a field-day. The *Field* in an editorial in November 1978 stated:

> The world of animal welfare produces some strange bed-fellows, or so it might appear at first glance. It seems that the British Horse Society is allied to the League Against Cruel Sports in wanting to put animals into politics.

The article commented on the campaign brochure and that the BHS as a member of the National Joint Equine Welfare Committee, had advised on the section dealing with protecting horses and ponies, and the League Against Cruel Sports had advised on the abolition of hunting and coursing. The article continued:

> The General Election Co-ordinating Committee is wise enough to publish a note at the start of the booklet pointing out that the Joint Consultative bodies are responsible only for the views expressed in the area of concern for which they are the advisory body.[3]

Later in February 1979, the *Field* reported the withdrawal of the Universities Federation for Animal Welfare under the headline *A*

Houghton Setback—The Universities Federation draw the line at politics. The *Shooting Times and Country Magazine* reported gleefully on the withdrawal of the British Horse Society and the RSPB from the campaign with the comment:

It can only be regretted that the Humane Education Council, in which the above mentioned societies put their good faith for the benefit of education in schools and colleges, should have apparently used the good names of such organisations to promote political ideas.[4]

It can only be assumed that certain organisations did not trouble to read the material sent to them in draft form from February 1978 onwards, relating to the campaign and the areas of concern we intended to cover. We also emphasised in our letter to the political parties that:

We must leave any choice of "priorities" to the judgment of the parties themselves. While we aim at "putting animals into politics" it is not for us to enter into discussion of the obvious political and electoral aspects of policy formation.

Leaving aside the six areas of concern, the main platform of the campaign was to gain acceptance from the political parties that animal welfare and protection was government responsibility and could no longer be left to the lottery and frustration of the Private Members' Bill procedure—an objective which every animal society in Britain should have been able to support.

CHAPTER XIII

The Party Conferences

Seaside towns in late autumn are the traditional setting for the political party conferences. In 1978, the curtain raiser was, as usual, the Liberal conference which was held in Southport from 11th to 16th September. Next came the Labour Party at Blackpool from 2nd to 6th October, followed closely by the Conservative Party in Brighton from 10th to 13th October.

GECCAP, in common with everyone else, had been unsure if the party conferences would take place in 1978, since all depended on the Prime Minister's decision on an autumn general election. However when Mr Callaghan made it clear that there was to be no autumn election, GECCAP considered it essential to have a strong presence at the party conferences, backed up by large-scale advertising in the press. The dramatic and immediate response from the League Against Cruel Sports to GECCAP's call for financial support enabled us to proceed with this plan and create quite a stir at the party conferences. Mr Richard Course, who had been seconded from the League to organise the information centres and fringe meetings at the conferences, Mr Brian Gunn, Assistant Secretary of the National Anti-Vivisection Society and subsequently Treasurer of GECCAP, Miss Joan Chambers of the League and the many voluntary helpers from the local branches of the societies were the unsung heroes of the conferences.

In order to appreciate the situation fully, it is helpful to have attended a political party conference. At each conference many pressure groups are present, representing all mannner of interests which are often in conflict with one another. The objective of the pressure groups is to reach the delegates and the objective of the organisers and stewards is to keep the pressure groups away from the delegates.

The obvious place to attract attention is at the entrance of conference centre, but this is often complicated by the fact that there is more than one entrance, as at the Winter Gardens in

Blackpool. In any event, delegates are being overwhelmed by leaflets, banners and placards as they arrive. Other less obvious tactics have to be employed, one of which is to gain admittance to the conference centre. There are usually two kinds of pass, one for delegates, which is virtually impossible to obtain, and the other for press and visitors, which is very difficult to obtain. The latter only permits entry to the gallery and not to the floor of the conference. Due to the enthusiasm and dogged persistence of our organisers, the campaign to "Put Animals Into Politics" succeeded in achieving this difficult feat.

During each of the party conferences, GECCAP inserted large advertisements in the newspapers likely to be read by delegates to that conference., (*Observer, Guardian, Daily Mirror* etc.) as well as advertising in the party journals and daily conference agendas. This was the first of two advertisement layouts used in the campaign. Without doubt, the most effective piece of local on-the-spot advertising was an enormous sign, mounted on an articulated lorry, which carried the message:

PUT ANIMALS INTO POLITICS
Animal Protection—Put it in the Manifesto

This was the idea of Dick Course. During the Labour Party conference, the lorry was parked at right-angles to the road in the forecourt of the Carlton Hotel which stands on the seafront at Blackpool only a few yards from the Imperial Hotel, the headquarters of the Labour Party. The Prime Minister, along with members of the Government and the National Executive Committee, saw the sign four times each day as they walked between their hotel and the conference centre. In addition, many thousands of visitors to Blackpool who had come to see the illuminations also saw our huge sign as they drove or walked along the promenade.

We were not so fortunate at the Conservative Party conference in Brighton, as the hotel we were using as the information centre had no forecourt. Dick Course therefore decided to drive the lorry around the town during the times that delegates were arriving and leaving the conference centre. This worked very well, due in part, perhaps, to regular breakdowns of the lorry right outside the centre and the Grand Hotel, the headquarters used by the Conservative Party.

We had organised a photographic and visual aid exhibition featuring the six areas of concern and linked to the national advertising. This exhibition was moved to each of the conference towns to form the main part of the information centre for the campaign. The information centre at Southport for the Liberal Party conference was at the Royal Clifton Hotel. Separate invitation cards were printed inviting delegates to visit the information centre and to attend the fringe meeting, and these were handed out to delegates during the week together with a leaflet on "Putting Animals Into Politics." A full page advertisement also appeared in the daily agenda inviting delegates to visit the information centre and attend the fringe meeting.

Delegates staying at the principal hotels had both invitation cards placed on their breakfast tables. This led to some complaints from hotel managers, but served its purpose in ensuring that delegates knew we were there. The fringe meeting was announced from the platform at the conference and in the event there was standing room only such was the support we had from the Liberal delegates.

Leafleting at the Labour Party conference at Blackpool was made difficult due to large crowds of demonstrators and sightseers outside the conference centre. Our indefatigable workers, however, had obtained one visitors pass, and by 10 a.m. on the first day of the conference, six helpers were inside the building. Even Dick Course was astonished to notice, on looking over the balcony, Brian Gunn and a voluntary helper sitting in the front row of the delegates, from where they proceeded to hand invitation cards to the Prime Minister, most of the Cabinet, and the National Executive Committee as they entered to mount the platform.

The fringe meeting was held in the Carlton Hotel where the information centre was also established. Robin Corbett chaired the meeting which once again was one of the best attended fringe meetings of the conference week.

The Daily Telegraph reported on GECCAP's efforts in Blackpool:

One of the most lavishly funded of the many pressure groups lobbying M.P.'s and delegates at Blackpool this week—the large number of which Mr. Callaghan referred to in his conference speech yesterday—is the General Election Co-ordinating

99

Committee for Animal Protection's campaign to "Put Animals Into Politics."

An umbrella organisation chaired by Lord Houghton and backed by sixty animal welfare groups as diverse as the RSPCA, Chickens' Lib and the Society for United Prayer for Animals, it will be mounting an even more intensive campaign for the Conservative conference next week.[1]

The reporter also referred to being offered a drink "from the Committee's well stocked bar." This comment led to a number of complaints from animal societies and supporters. Anyone, however, who has had any experience of trying to attract delegates to a meeting, or for that matter the press will know that "a well-stocked bar" is the best inducement you can offer. It is not a question of wasting the hard-earned money of the animal welfare movement on high living, but rather using the money to achieve the best results.

The Conservative meeting at Brighton was covered in a similar manner. Invitations were delivered to delegates outside the conference centre and under the bedroom doors at the principal hotels. Mrs Thatcher and leading shadow ministers had several invitations given to them. Most accepted with good grace, although Mr Ted Heath became a little angry with our well behaved, polite but insistent distributors. The fringe meeting held at the Bedford Hotel was well attended and Mr James Prior was one very interested M.P. who visited the centre. Strong opposition was voiced by some of those attending, but there was also considerable support for the objectives of the campaign. Many of those attending were particularly outspoken over the proposed cull of the grey seal in Scottish waters which was receiving considerable press coverage at that time.

A newspaper correspondent attending one of the political party conferences said that the slogan "Putting Animals Into Politics" was misplaced. He added:

There are too many animals in politics already. There were snakes in the grass, leopards who cannot change their spots; elephants who never forget and lots of Parliamentarians who think they are the cat's whiskers.

100

A Grey seal and pup.
The Secretary of State for Scotland was forced to abandon the larger part of a proposed cull of grey seals in the Orkneys in 1978 due to public opinion.

Hare Coursing.

This bedraggled kitten was rescued from the River Thames.

This handsome cat is the same animal—after a year of loving care.

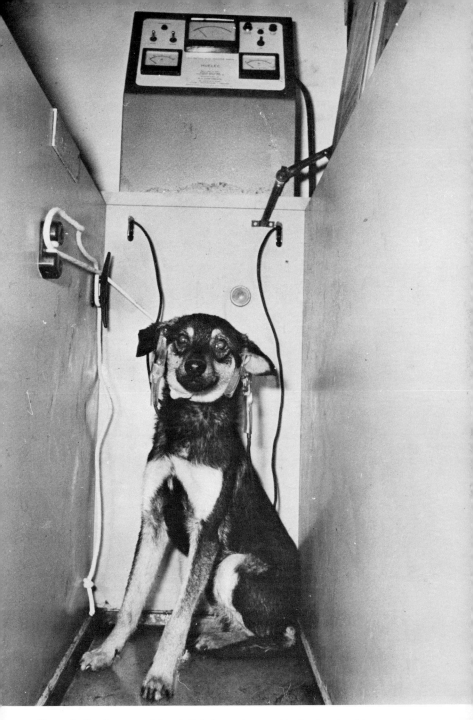

The majority of unwanted dogs in Britain are destroyed in the electric cabinet —a sad death for an unwanted pet.

"The price of a sealskin coat".
A 'whitecoat' baby harp seal being clubbed to death in the Gulf of St. Lawrence.

This comment was included in an article by Lord Houghton in the *Contemporary Review*. In this article, Lord Houghton said of the campaign's coverage of the party conferences:

> This proved to be a particularly worthwhile exercise. We were able to gauge delegates' reaction to the campaign and were happily surprised by the numbers who attended our fringe meetings. The support we received at all three conferences proved that whatever their respective parties decided to do in the field of animal welfare, many delegates were very much aware of the growing public disquiet on matters of animal abuse and exploitation. [2]

A great deal of time, effort and hard work went into the political party conferences, and at the end of the day the GECCAP organisers and voluntary workers went home convinced that no delegate to any of the party conferences was unaware of the campaign to "Put Animals Into Politics."

After all the excitement of the party conferences, we came to the end of the year still not knowing when the general election would take place. But we did know it must come in 1979. We sent out our first newsletter to the societies and supporters at the turn of the year, when we were able to report on the response from the political parties to our discussion document:

> *CONSERVATIVE PARTY*: The Committee is in correspondence with Lord Thorneycroft, Chairman of the Conservative Party, and informal contacts lead us to hope that a meeting can be arranged in the near future with the Policy-making Committee of the Party to discuss our proposals in detail. The Party has already expressed concern over the usage of animals for experimentation.

> *LABOUR PARTY*: The Labour Party's response is set out in detail in their Policy Document—"Living Without Cruelty—Labour's Charter for Animal Protection." [3]

> This is a comprehensive policy statement on Animal Welfare, including experiments with live animals, transportation, export of food animals, factory farming, dogs and pets, zoos, wildlife parks, circuses and blood sports.

101

LIBERAL PARTY: At a meeting of the Liberal Party Council on 25th November, two resolutions on animal welfare were accepted by an overwhelming majority. These resolutions included acceptance of both the principles set out in our policy document and further called for urgent action on vivisection, factory farming, export of livestock, the abuses of artificial herbicides, fungicides and insecticides, other pollution on sea and on land and for the registration of dogs. These resolutions have now become official Liberal Party policy.

PLAID CYMRU: We are still waiting to hear from the National Executive Committee of Plaid Cymru on the proposals set forth in our discussion document.

SCOTTISH NATIONAL PARTY: At a meeting with representatives of the Scottish National Party in September, the Party accepted the two basic principles and the following resolution on the principles and areas of concern will be tabled at their national Party conference in May:—

This Party affirms that one of the standards of a civilised society is the protection from unnecessary suffering which it affords to animals.

We believe that animal welfare must be a matter of public policy and, therefore, should not be left primarily to the lottery of Private Members' Bills as has frequently been the practice of the Westminster Parliament. We support the establishment of a standing commission or an all-party standing specialist committee of the legislature to make a continuing review of existing legislation and its implementation and to make recommendations for legislative or administrative changes where this appears necessary.

The following areas are ones which we feel in particular require review:

1. Experiments on living animals, especially those carried out for non-medical purposes.
2. Conditions in intensive animal husbandry.
3. The control of dogs in the community.
4. Wild life conservation.
5. Export of live food animals.

At this stage the Labour Party had gone further than any of the other parties in nailing their colours to the mast. Their policy document, *Living Without Cruelty*, was a brave attempt by a political party to come to grips with a difficult area of policy in which many vested interests were involved. The statement did not lack punch:

> At present Britain tolerates far too much unnecessary suffering among wild life; the animals and other species who provide our food, domestic pets and animals in captivity. The legislation which is supposed to protect them from cruelty is often defective and inadequately enforced. The time has come to bring it up to the standards of which we can be proud.

However, in spite of this policy statement, there was no guarantee that the Labour Party or any of the other parties would include animal welfare and protection in their manifestos. For our part we concluded our first News Letter with the comment:

> We enter the election year fully prepared and with high hopes of success. What actually goes into the election manifestos will be decided very soon—and that is our task for 1979.

CHAPTER XIV

Continuing Action and Political Debate

The campaign to put animals into politics was now really getting into its stride. In the summer of 1978, we had written individually to all the animal welfare organisations in Britain informing them of what we had done and asking for their active support as soon as the political parties responded to our letter:

> We shall then need your help. We cannot stress too much the crucial importance of this first attempt to mobilise a combined effort of the "animal lobby" to put animal protection in the party manifestos. We must be quick and we must be bold and we must keep our minds on the target all the time. We aim to mobilise the most impressive demonstration of unity and strength the animal societies have ever presented to politicians and Parliament.

This was followed by a further letter in which we asked local societies and branches of national organisations, particularly in those areas with marginal constituencies, to approach the local constituency associations of all the political parties asking for their support.

The *Scotsman* ran an article on why marginals became pressure points in an election and used "Putting Animals Into Politics" as an illustration:

> Directed from Edinburgh, the Group have issued a campaign handbook with a little map showing the location of some 40 British constituencies held on less than 1000 votes. Activists are advised that "it is our supporters in the marginal constituencies who we rely upon to bring maximum pressure to bear on candidates." It is here they are told, where they will have "greater effect on the outcome of the election" and where "the media will pay more attention." [1]

We also wrote to all the trade unions and student bodies asking for support for the campaign. A special letter addressed to Members of Parliament, together with the campaign brochure, was inserted in the *House Magazine* for delivery to M.P.'s and peers. The *Veterinary Record* refused to accept a campaign brochure and covering letter addressed to vets and so we mailed the letter and poster to every vet in private practice in Britain, asking them to display the poster in their waiting rooms. Many vets were sympathetic and a number asked for supplies of the brochure and car stickers. Others were not so sympathetic. One reply ran:

I suppose that most vets will be too busy or too idle to reply to you and I fear that you may take this silence as consent. So in case you think you have the unanimous approval of the profession, please note that I disagree with you and would certainly vote against any parliamentary candidate who espoused your cause.

The campaign's first national advertising was timed to coincide with the political party conferences. It was clear that the general election would now be in the spring of 1979 or the autumn of that year. The new electoral registers would not be operative until mid-February and the Scottish and Welsh referenda were being held on 1st March, therefore a March election seemed unlikely. Local government elections were planned for May and the elections for the European Parliament were to be held on 7th June; July and August are not usually election months due to the holiday season. Therefore, unless the Government intended to remain in office until the statutory end of the Parliament in October, the likely date for the general election appeared to be April 1979.

Our advertising agency, Espley and Espley Advertising Limited took the view that between the conference advertising and the final burst of national advertising immediately prior to the election, we needed to place specialised low-key advertising in magazines and journals to keep the campaign in the minds of the public. For this reason it was agreed that between February and April the campaign should take space in religious, educational, political and opinion-forming journals.

The RSPCA did not provide any direct funding for this campaign, but it did set aside fifty thousand pounds to support advertising for the campaign, subject to such advertising material being approved by a sub-committee of the RSPCA Council. This requirement was largely to protect the RSPCA's charitable status. This grant came too late for use in the first series of advertisements in September and October and we obtained agreement from the Council to use up to ten thousand pounds for itemised expenditure to be approved by the Council, since at this time funds were needed to cover such matters as printing costs and the production of car-stickers rather than advertising.

Subsequently Lord Houghton and I attended a meeting of the RSPCA sub-committee appointed to approve the specialised interim advertising and the planned national advertising for the run-up to the general election. This was not the happiest of meetings and both Lord Houghton and I were aware of an air of resentment on the part of certain members of the sub-committee. At one stage, a member of the committee complained that the formation of GECCAP had been unnecessary since the RSPCA was quite capable of running a political campaign. This statement was, of course, quite true, but the point was that the RSPCA had not taken the initiative and organised such a campaign.

During this period when the country was waiting to learn when the election would take place, there was growing activity all over the country in support of the campaign by societies, branches, groups (many of them old Animal Welfare Year groups) and individuals. Mr Brian Gunn and a group of volunteers canvassed the Young Conservative conference in February and succeeded in placing leaflets on every seat in the auditorium and the platform before the delegates arrived. Mrs Fay Funnell, who later gained considerable press coverage for publicly burning a fur-coat she purchased at the Debenham sale, distributed literature at a Liberal Party rally in Farnborough with another group of volunteers. Local constituency associations, prospective parliamentary candidates, Members of Parliament and government ministers were being bombarded with letters from supporters asking what their party intended doing about animals. GECCAP also decided at this time to hold a series of "tea-time" meetings in the House of Commons for the three major parties, so that we could make direct contact with sympathetic members ourselves. These meetings, sponsored by members from the three parties were particularly valuable for a number of reasons, not least being the idea to form "ginger" groups within each of the main political parties, to work, as it were, from the inside.

At this stage in the campaign we had a stroke of good fortune. Mr Jeff Rooker, M.P. for Birmingham, Perry Barr, was successful in the ballot for Private Members' Motions and as a result was able to obtain a full day debate in the House of Commons on animal welfare, which he linked to "Putting Animals Into Politics." [2] The debate, which took place on 23rd March 1979, was opened by Mr Rooker who summed up the reasons which made it necessary to put animals into politics:

> The animal welfare societies as a whole have realised in the last eighteen months or so that they must begin to use the political process as ruthlessly as does any other lobby operating in a democracy—whether that lobby relates to poverty, housing or environmental matters. The animal welfare societies have decided that they must combine their efforts. In the last year, particularly following Animal Welfare Year, when many such societies combined effectively for the first time, their efforts have been quite successful.

Mr Rooker went on to outline a number of areas of concern where action was needed to alleviate the suffering inflicted upon animals. He concluded his speech by referring to the Standing Royal Commission sought by GECCAP and the statement made by the Prime Minister the previous day on the Government's intention to set up a Council of Animal Welfare. [3] Mr Rooker did not want to quibble about words and was not concerned about the title of the body to be set up. All that he wanted was that the body "should have sufficient weight behind it." He went on to spell out exactly what he meant:

> The animal welfare organisations should be represented on it in the majority. I want no nonsense about a "balance of interests." This body will be concerned with animal welfare, not animal use. I shall be most upset and annoyed if the animal welfare organisations are not in the majority on the Council. They must be, in order to make it effective.

Sir David Renton, Conservative Member for Huntingdonshire, was the next speaker. Sir David assured the House that he agreed with a number of points made by Mr Rooker and especially on experiments on animals, but on other issues he could not agree and emphasised:

The subject of animal welfare is a vast scenario of conflicting interests, strong human emotions, elaborate but sometimes inadequate administration and potentially stringent but partly unenforcable legislation.

Sir David did not agree with the setting up of another "quango." What was needed instead, he said:

Is action by the Government, with or without new legislative powers. I hope that the next Conservative Government will get on with this problem.

Mr Arthur Latham, Labour Member for Paddington, spoke with some passion on attitudes:

Some people care nothing about animals and regard them as objects, things that are expendable and there to eat, skin, hunt, experiment with, vivisect and be available for human exploitation and enjoyment regardless of suffering. They think that animals have no rights.

The next speaker was Mr F. A. Burden, Conservative Member for Gillingham and Chairman of the Parliamentary Animal Welfare Group. In his speech Mr Burden said:

The slogan "Putting Animals into Politics" has recently been coined and publicised by a body calling itself the General Election Co-ordinating Committee for Animal Protection. That slogan implies that animal welfare has never been in party politics before. That is untrue.

Mr Burden referred to his record in the House since 1950 and paid tribute to other members, no longer in the House, to whom animal welfare had been an important issue. He then referred to the record of Conservative governments in this field. Mr Burden believed that "animal welfare is in the forefront of politics" and that:

It is fictitious and misleading to imply that animal welfare is only now being put into party politics as a result of the activities and slogan of the General Election Co-ordinating Committee

109

for Animal Protection. I hope that animal welfare will basically remain a non-party issue.

Mr John Silkin, then Minister of Agriculture, Fisheries and Food, spoke on the Government's announcement to set up a Council for Animal Welfare. The Council would have three standing committees and the power to promote other standing committees as and when a topic became necessary. The three standing committees would be the two existing advisory committees, the Farm Animal Welfare Advisory Committee and the Home Office Committee on the 1876 Act, and a new Committee on the transport of farm animals whether it was for slaughter, breeding or fattening. Mr Silkin concluded by saying:

> A civilised government look after the helpless in the community and those who cannot help themselves, whether they are old, sick, disabled or children—or animals, which are not able, except through the friends that they have among mankind, to make their own responses to their needs.

Mr Peter Mills, Conservative Member for Devon West, spoke from the Opposition front bench and summarised the Conservative view on animal welfare in his concluding remarks:

> I should like to sum up so that no one can say that we have not stated our views clearly: I know that people tend to forget what has been said before. We shall act as quickly as possible fully to support the new measures of the community. That must be done. We shall update Brambell and the codes of welfare for farm animals. We shall update the legislation on experiments on live animals. We shall examine the working of the export of live animals and we shall call a halt to the export of old cows and ewes recently calved and lambed.

> We Conservatives believe that these are sensible positive, steps and are the right way forward for animal welfare.

Mr Robin Corbett, Labour Member for Hemel Hempstead and Chairman of the FAWCE, expressed his disappointment over "the negative attitude that has been taken in relation to the Council for Animal Welfare which the Prime Minister announced yesterday." Mr Corbett discussed four major areas of concern, live exports of food animals, the trade in horses, performing animals, and experiments on living animals. The new Council, he said should discuss these matters and discuss them in the open:

There have been too many closed doors in this area for too long. Every one of those doors needs ripping from its hinges to encourage those who are concerned and have opinions on these matters to come to the new Council to debate and discuss the issue in the open where statements can be challenged and evidence cross-examined. Only if the Council operates in that way will it be seen as a proper response to the sustained and growing concern over animal welfare.

Mr Stephen Hastings, Conservative Member for Mid-Bedfordshire, complained that: "It is a shame to insert into this debate a political attack on legitimate and legal country sports. . . ." He also referred to the brochure, *Putting Animals Into Politics*, of which he said:

It places field sports as the main target. It purports to carry the support of a wide, large and varied list of organisations, some of which did not realise that their names were being used in this context.

Mr Hastings went on to list the names of the organisations which had withdrawn support and, perhaps without realising what he was doing, he confirmed the real reason for their action.

It was totally untrue to say that field sports were the main target of the campaign. Our main target was to gain acceptance by the political parties that animal welfare and protection was a government responsibility and could no longer be left to the lottery of the Private Members' Bill procedure and also to promote the establishment of a Standing Royal Commission on Animal Protection. We then included six areas of concern of which hunting with hounds was only one and we emphasised in our brochure:

Included, therefore, with our letter was an Appendix listing six main areas of concern on which our member societies invited political parties to make statements of policy. (N.B. These areas of concern are not listed in any order of priority).

111

It was also incorrect to say that some of the organisations listed did not realise that their names were being used in this context. The draft letter to the political parties was sent out to all the organisations involved.

Mr Andrew Bennett, Labour Member for Stockport North, did not mince his words over the proposed Council for Animal Welfare:

> I expect the body to produce action. The Council must be independent from those who, unfortunately, make profits out of cruelty. That fact must be stressed. It must not be talking shop or an excuse for delaying action.

Miss Janet Fookes, Conservative Member for Plymouth Drake, and now Chairman of the RSPCA Council, welcomed the Government's proposal to set up a Council for Animal Welfare and stressed:

> I hope that people will be picked (to serve on the Council) not simply because they represent an organisation but because they have expertise in their particular field and, at the same time, have a known commitment to animal welfare.

Miss Fookes was most outspoken on the subject of the live export of food animals and believed the time had come to ban the trade:

> All attempts to enforce those regulations have failed. Why, therefore, should we be asked to put faith in the tightening up of regulations, when the current regulations are not working?

Mr Ronald Atkins, Labour Member for Preston North, informed the House why the animal societies were determined to put animals into politics:

> They (the societies) have tried for long enough to get results by other means, and now they have rightly decided that it should become an election issue.

Mr Stephen Ross, Liberal Member for the Isle of Wight, made a plea for the plight of whales, the Canadian harp seal, and our own grey seal. He made a very valid point on organised culling:

> The real problem is that all these animals—seals, and wild birds in particular—are in grave danger from oil pollution. We do not

112

need to do much to cull them because, unfortunately, they will surely die from oil pollution.

Mr Ross could not accept the argument against hunting although he did not hunt himself. The next speaker Mr Arnold Shaw, Labour Member for Ilford South, argued:

Whatever is said about the welfare of animals, one thing is certain—no argument can justify the pursuit and killing of animals for pleasure.

Mr Shaw was followed by Mr Marcus Kimball, Conservative Member for Gainsborough, who predictably did not quite see eye to eye with Mr Shaw:

Having listened to a very inaccurate and misleading speech by the honourable Member for Ilford South, (Mr Shaw) I find myself welcoming the idea of a Council, if it will get rid of such ignorant speeches and such ignorant views as we have heard expressed on the subject of field sports. Field sports have nothing to fear from the setting up of the Council.

Mr John Watkinson, Labour Member for Gloucestershire West, could not associate himself with the remarks of the previous speaker and then concentrated on the gassing of badgers by the Ministry in an attempt to control bovine tuberculosis. He concluded his speech with the plea:

The badger is one of the friendliest and most beloved of wild creatures. I simply ask "Are we giving a square deal to the badger?"

Mr Jasper More, Conservative Member for Ludlow, had some harsh words to say about the hunt saboteurs, but nothing to say about the hunt "heavies," who are not involved in disrupting hunts, but rather in damaging the hunt saboteurs:

After all the ill-informed statements about field sports, I would add that the organised confrontations at field sports meetings—obviously organised by saboteurs, sometimes brought from a long distance—are disgraceful. They also simply divert the police from their proper duties.

113

Mr Tony Newton, Conservative Member for Braintree, welcomed the debate and gave the motion his full support, but regretted that some Members had sought to turn the debate from a political issue into a party political issue. Mr Robert Boscawen, Conservative Member for Wells, rounded off the debate and made particular reference to pets and public and private zoos.

The Under Secretary of State for the Home Department, Dr Shirley Summerskill, replied to the debate on behalf of the Government. In her speech, which referred in the main to the Government's proposal to set up the Council for Animal Welfare, Dr Summerskill made a very pointed comment which all animal welfare organisations should consider very carefully:

> There are strong differences of opinion between animal welfare bodies on many issues. If the Council can achieve some unanimity, which can be shared by this House, that will be a great step forward.

It had been an exciting debate, and in this respect Mr Phillip Whitehead, Labour Member for Derby North, echoed the feelings of many of us:

> Regardless of our party, age and experience in the House, we can say that this is a great day for animal welfare.

CHAPTER XV

The Importance of Publicity from the "Opposition"

There was no shortage of publicity during the campaign to put animals into politics. Pat Chapman of Animal Advocates Information Service acted as the clearing house for information and handled the press releases put out during the campaign by GECCAP. Partly owing to the national advertising campaign, however, and partly owing to the tremendous response and support from the public, publicity was largely self-generating. Newspapers and journals throughout Britain reported on putting animals into politics and radio and television also provided excellent coverage. In a report which emphasised that "there were a lot of votes to be won in four-legged politics," the *Economist* commented on the campaign and observed that "in the past 18-months there has been a revolution in the animal lobby: the fuddy-duddies and the foxhunters have been kicked out and replaced by young activists." [1]

But what was particularly interesting was the reaction of the "opposition" newspapers and journals. When the "opposition" comes out on the defensive, I am more than pleased. In the past, farming journals and the scientific press have devoted little space to animal welfare campaigns simply because they posed no threat. However, "Putting Animals Into Politics" was covered very widely in such journals. The reports and articles were often critical, but the defensive stance adopted indicated in my view, the growing concern of such organisations to a unified campaign which was achieving results.

I have used the word opposition in quotes because I personally do not believe that, for example, the National Farmers' Union should be considered as being in opposition to the welfare cause: we should be on the same side. *Poultry World* referred to this aspect in a report on the campaign:

Secretary of the Committee, Clive Hollands explained that the target of any proposed campaign would not be to make life difficult for farmers, but rather to try and find some realistic and feasible approach to the situation. [2]

In an earlier issue, *Poultry World* devoted four pages to two articles under the title, *Animal Welfare—Who Pays*? The first, written by Gerry Emmans of the East of Scotland College of Agriculture, argued that the poultry industry should be merely an interested spectator as the real battle was fought between poultry workers' representatives and consumers. His main point was that new systems may be idyllic for hens—at least in the view of welfarists—but that eggs would cost more (hence the interest of consumers) and it was unlikely that the jobs and working conditions would be ideal for the people (hence the interest of the poultry workers' representatives).

The second article was by Dr David Sainsbury of the University of Cambridge, who suggested that the only way to bring the extreme stances of welfarists and industry together was to develop a broader view on research:

> I am convinced that we need a separate establishment or unit to give the proper prominence to the question of co-ordinating and studying livestock welfare, considering alternative systems and relating those to the better use of the world's resources. [3]

The *Farmers Guardian* gave front-page headlines to what the editor called a *New Attack on 'factory farming' and Exports*, [4] while the *Farmers Weekly* adopted a more restrained headline: *Drive to Put Animals into Election Politics*. [5]

Insight, a journal of the National Farmers' Union, carried a whole series of articles on welfare in one issue. In one of these articles, *Brambell and Beyond*, the author, Trevor Parfitt, referred to Ruth Harrison serving on a European committee as an example of the fact that British animal welfare lobbyists were moving into Europe, where Mrs Harrison, he said, could be relied upon "to keep stirring the pot":

> If they succeeed in their efforts to 'bring animals into politics' in the U.K., there are those in Europe who will watch with interest. So far the other Common Market countries are not het up about the subject but there are enough indications of concern for the

other member organisations of COPA to have started taking notice.

This statement emphasises the importance of British animal welfare activity, as this is one area where other countries watch to see what happens here. Mr Parfitt concluded his article with this observation:

> What was far from clear in 1964, and seems still to be indistinct now, is why so many British people appear to prefer to take up what they think to be injustice to animals rather than directing their energies to the needs of their fellow humans. [6]

How many animal welfare workers have had that thrown at them when on the public platform? It certainly has come my way on many occasions, usually from those who know no better. The majority of people whom I have known who work in the field of animal welfare, also work for the benefit of humans and those who make the accusation frequently work neither for the welfare of animals nor the welfare of man. The quote above however was from the Director of the Consumer Affairs Division of the National Farmers Union and from someone who should have known better.

The *Veterinary Record* commented on the campaign in an editorial, *Animal Welfare in the Political Arena*:

> It is quite right that politicians and those seeking to influence them should be involved with animal welfare matters. There are indeed abuses which are of long standing and require new or amended legislation to correct. [7]

It was, however, that magazine popular with the county set, the *Field* which gave the campaign a major boost, much to the pleasure of Lord Houghton and myself. Under the title, *Putting Animals into Politics—Behind the Campaign and the Dangers it poses to the Future of Field Sports*, the report dealt in depth with the campaign and the working of the animal welfare societies:

> Most animal welfare groups use lawful means to further their ends and strive to win support in Parliament for their aims. They pursue notoriously separate paths, however. Several groups with similar aims may campaign quite separately and dissipate the strength of the welfare movement.

A determined and professional effort has now been made to unite them all behind the slogan Putting Animals into Politics.

The fact that so many different organisations could work together appeared to surprise the *Field*:

> Merely to persuade that vast assortment to be listed together marks a formidable achievement of persuasion and administration by Lord Houghton and his colleagues. . . .
> . . . .If Lord Houghton keeps his disparate crew together for the next general election he will have a lobby of formidable and potential resources. The election period is the target of his campaign.

The article warned readers of the effective nature of the campaign:

> Many statements of intent by voluntary campaigning groups sound like the rallying cries of crusaders. Lord Houghton's booklet is couched in careful terms in which the Parliamentary or statutory background to welfare campaigns is always stressed. He makes it impossible for his organisation to be dismissed as a group of naive enthusiasts with more passion than impact. If his co-ordinating effort is successful it will mark a very large step forward for what are often described collectively as 'the caring societies.' There is certainly no comparable structure to present counter argument.

The last sentence of the above quote gives the clue to the real concern of the *Field*, which is stated clearly in the concluding paragraph of the article:

> Lord Houghton's initiative is a serious challenge to all who are concerned with hunting hounds. They have little time in which to rally to meet it, no matter for how long the Prime Minister postpones the election date.[8]

Another article of interest was a contribution by Bill McMillan in the *Nursing Times*. The article, aptly titled, *Vivisection—Do we have Double Standards?* was concerned with the vivisection issue and presented a reasoned, if somewhat biased statement from a man who is employed by the Chemical Industries Association and is a member of the Research Defence Society. The *Nursing Times* gave space in the same issue for two other articles, one by Alan

Whittaker, at that time General Secretary of the British Union for the Abolition of Vivisection, and the other by Julie Eagles, a senior staff nurse at St. Bartholomew's Hospital. Miss Eagles provided an insight into nurses' views:

> Most nurses with whom I have discussed the subject of vivisection agree that if the experiment is for medical research they are in favour, providing that the animal is humanely treated, does not unduly suffer and is destroyed after the experiment.

She also commented:

> Despite the strict rules and regulations governing this practice, some animals are still being used in useless, non-vital, non-medical experiments, and are grossly and inhumanely treated.

To return, however, to Mr McMillan's article in which he also referred to Animal Welfare Year and the political campaigns. In this article he wrote:

> A special publicity effort was made during 1976, the Centenary of the Cruelty to Animals Act, under which this work (vivisection) is conducted. More recently an expensive advertising campaign, reported to be costing over £100,000 lumps animal experimentation with blood sports and the export of live animals in an effort to put animals into politics. One wonders how many kidney machines for humans such sums of money could buy. [9]

I have some respect for Mr McMillan, but this snide comment must be reported and answered. This is precisely what Lord Houghton did in a letter published in the *Nursing Times*:

> Of course we have double standards not only about animals but about women, illegitimate children, coloured people and living in sin. . . . We are rarely rational or logical about anything which touches our emotions or prejudices. Sheer lunacy is tolerated if it can be called 'conscience.'

Lord Houghton went on to say that just as we have been trying to rid ourselves of double standards about humans, so we are now aiming to rid ourselves of double standard about animals:

It is no longer defensible to deny all rights to every other species except our own. This is an abuse of power.

Coming to the matter of expenditure on the campaign to put animals into politics, Lord Houghton did not pull his punches:

As for the budget of the campaign of the Co-ordinating Committee of which I am Chairman, we are spending pocket money compared with the money the tobacco industry is spending to merchandise the cause of lung cancer; or the brewers to merchandise the cause of alcoholism; or indeed the pharmaceutical industry to push substances down the throats of animals until they die, and others into the eyes of rabbits until they suffer, in order to sell the idea of beauty without regard to cruelty.

How many hospitals could be built with all that![10]

CHAPTER XVI

The General Election

Immediately the date of the general election was announced following the Government defeat on a vote of confidence, GECCAP issued its second newsletter. In this newsletter we asked all the societies, groups and individual supporters to make even greater efforts to put animals into politics since we were now entering the most important phase of the campaign as the election manifestos of the parties would be published in the immediate future. A number of questions were posed:

Will the parties see the animal welfare issue as being sufficiently important to warrant reference being made to it in the election manifestos?

Will the parties state that they will support the setting up of the proposed Council for Animal Welfare?

Will the parties commit themselves on specific areas of concern as discussed in our brochure Put Animals Into Politics?

Personal contact with candidates and local constituency associations was now of prime importance, as were efforts to gain publicity in the press and on local radio and television. Attendance at candidates meetings during the hustings to ask questions on animal welfare issues and to ascertain candidates' personal views as well as the party's views on GECCAP's proposals, was the kind of supporting action that everyone could take.

The Committee had to be very careful at this time not to encourage or permit any supporter to contravene the *Representation of the People Act, 1949.* This Act requires that during a parliamentary election (that is from the date of the dissolution of Parliament or any earlier time at which the Queen's intention to dissolve Parliament is announced, until the close of the poll) no expense shall be incurred by any person other than the candidate, or by persons acting with his authority, in such matters as holding public meetings, or other forms of canvassing on the candidates behalf. It would therefore be an offence to urge electors to vote for a particular candidate or party because of their support for animal welfare measures, or not to vote for a candidate or party because of lack of support. This issue was particularly relevant during the 1979 general election since at a by-election in March 1978, the Director of the Society for the Protection of the Unborn Child was sent to trial at Snaresbrook Crown Court accused of improperly issuing pamphlets which could have affected the outcome of a by-election. [1]

I believe that the success of the campaign to put animals into politics can be measured by the fact that the three major political parties in Britain all included animal welfare and protection in their election manifestos for the first time in the history of the British Parliament. This is what the parties said in their manifestos:

Conservative Party:
The welfare of animals is an issue that concerns us all. There are problems in certain areas and we will act immediately where it is necessary. More specifically, we will give full support to the EEC proposals on the transportation of animals. We shall update the Brambell Report, the codes of welfare for farm animals, and the legislation on experiments on live animals. We shall also re-examine the rules and enforcement applying to the export of live animals and shall halt the export of cows and ewes recently calved and lambed.

Labour Party:
Under Labour' new Council for Animal Welfare we will have stronger control on the export of live animals for export, on conditions of factory farms and on experiments on living animals.

Legislation to end cruelty to animals will include the banning of hare-coursing and stag and deer hunting. Angling and shooting will in no way be affected by our proposals.

Liberal Party:
Support the demand of the General Election Co-ordinating Committee for Animal Protection for a Royal Commission on Animal Welfare. Ban the importation and manufacture of any

product derived from any species whose survival is threatened, and work for a total ban on commercial whaling.

We also need a co-ordinated approach to the needs of food production and conservation of natural wildlife which recognises their interdependence.

Increase the number of abattoirs to EEC standard to discourage the export of live animals.

The action of support groups and individuals during the run-up to the general election was quite staggering. A group in Gravesend in Kent hired a double-decker bus and toured around the Medway towns, stopping in all the shopping centres to disembark the voluntary workers who then proceeded to hand out leaflets to shoppers. The East Midlands HSA distributed over forty-five thousand leaflets, while a group in Brighton covered nearly every house in the city. In Manchester another group covered large areas of the city with thirty thousand leaflets and car stickers. In all, half-a-million leaflets were handed out during the campaign as well as seventy-five thousand brochures, one hundred thousand car-stickers and ten thousand posters. All this activity was backed by full-scale advertising in the national and provincial press, with special emphasis on the local press in areas with marginal constituencies. For this final burst of advertising we used the second of the two layouts prepared by the agency.

We believed that we had done all that was possible with the funds available to ensure that all candidates standing for election to Parliament in the 1979 general election were made aware of the strength of public opinion on matters relating to the welfare and protection of animals.

The British Field Sports Society obviously viewed the campaign with some misgivings, since the Director of the BFSS wrote to all his members to draw their attention to this serious danger to field sports.

After listing the commitments of the three major parties on field (blood) sports, the letter urged all field sportsmen to use their power to the greatest effect in support of all their sports and urged members to tell other field sportsmen about the threat and to question parliamentary candidates about their stand on this issue. This letter followed shortly after some interesting letters stolen from the BFSS offices came to light. The letters in question were left on the doorstep of Mr Richard Course, who was later acquitted at the Inner London Crown Court of dishonestly receiving stolen documents.

The *Guardian* published a report on the trial and also revealed the contents of some of the letters. The *Guardian* reported that the letters disclosed a plot to discredit a Labour minister, a plan to "get at" Mrs Thatcher through her sister, and a claim that the BBC had guaranteed air time for the Society's views. [2]

The effect of the BFSS campaigning during the election had little or no effect on the campaign to put animals into politics, since our areas of concern were much wider than just the blood sports issue. A more serious matter was the totally unexpected action by the RSPCA in announcing their "Charter for Animals." This campaign was suddenly launched in the run-up to the general election and with no prior discussion or consultation with GECCAP. The charter, published in the form of an eight-page booklet, confused candidates and supporters alike since it adopted a rather different line from the "Put Animals Into Politics" brochure.

The charter certainly urged government to accept responsibility for animal welfare, calling for the setting up of a standing commission, but went on to propose the appointment of a senior minister to have responsibility for all animal welfare issues. This was not proposed by GECCAP, quite simply because we did not believe that it would work in practice.

In the areas of concern in the RSPCA charter, there were also differences with GECCAP. The charter set out four priority areas:

1. *Companion Animals*, particular importance being attached to methods of population control and to the introduction of trained dog wardens.

2. *Farm Animals*, with particular reference to cruelties involved in certain intensive systems and to the transport, export and slaughter of food animals.

3. *Animal Experimentation*, with particular emphasis on reducing both the total number of experiments which are carried out and the numbers and suffering of such animals as are in fact used in these experiments.

124

4.   *Wild Animals*, with particular reference to animals in zoos, exploited species and the use of traps, snares and poisons in the control of wild animals.

These were all important areas of concern and duplicated in the main the six areas of the GECCAP campaign, but they were to some extent different in approach and therefore confused the issue. The RSPCA also sent out a questionnaire to parliamentary candidates which again added to the confusion, as candidates were receiving RSPCA questionnaires and at the same time letters and direct questioning from GECCAP supporters.

As one Honorary Secretary of an RSPCA branch wrote to me:

I note with misgivings that the RSPCA charter-statement in the latest issue of RSPCA *Today* is verbose, insufficiently specific, overlaps only partly with GECCAP's main subjects and looks to me quite likely to blur candidates' impressions of what needs to be done.

I am afraid that I must agree with this view. It is a pity, that for whatever reason the decision was taken to launch the RSPCA charter, no consultation or discussion took place with GECCAP.

The decision by the Council of the League Against Cruel Sports to make a direct donation to the Labour Party Election Fund of eighty thousand pounds also created quite a stir in animal welfare circles, the repercussions of which are still being felt. The League took this decision quite independently and without reference to GECCAP, and it was the first entry into party politics by an animal welfare organisation. GECCAP had from the beginning remained totally non-party political and had approached all the political parties, whatever their colour, to ask for their support.

This donation was one of the largest, if not the largest single donation made to the Labour Party's Election Fund, apart from the grants made by some of the bigger Trade Unions and it soon resulted in a storm of protest. Although GECCAP had to cope with some of the backlash, I believe the League's action was justified. The main objective of the LACS, after all, is to abolish hunting and the Labour Party in their election manifesto was the only party to give any undertaking on this issue, stating, as it did, that "legislation to end cruelty to animals will include the banning of hare-coursing and stag and deer hunting."

The members of the League also took this view when they voted in support of the Council's action at an extraordinary general meeting in July 1979. This vote was further confirmed in a postal ballot when the membership voted overwhelmingly in favour of the Council.

When the general election was over, we sent out a final newsletter to everyone who had supported the campaign, pointing out that it was now a Conservative Government which would have the responsibility for animal welfare, possibly for the next five years. So the task now was to ensure that the Conservative Government lived up to the pledges made in their election manifesto. Making the right noises would not be enough—the animal welfare movement would want to see real action.

The last effective act of GECCAP was to complete the organisation of "ginger" groups within each of the three main political parties. We had made a start on this following the House of Commons "tea-parties." Strangely, the only group to be in action prior to the election was the one within the Conservative Party, the reason being that the election followed so quickly after the tea parties that there was insufficient time to organise Labour and Liberal groups. Early on in the campaign, however, we had been approached by an organisation known as the Conservative Ecology Group which offered GECCAP support and indeed produced some excellent papers. The most important of these was *The Case for Animal Reform*, in which the Group commented on all our areas of concern, including blood sports and stated:

> We intend to co-operate closely with responsible animal welfare organisations and we have already pledged our full support to GECCAP, the General Election Co-ordinating Committee for Animal Protection, which comprises sixty-five charities and groups.

This paper, along with two others, *Animal Protection—A Political Issue* and *Experiments on Living Animals*, were sent out by the group to all Conservative M.P.'s and other members in the Party. "Ginger" groups are now also operating effectively in both the Labour Party and the Liberal Party.

At the Meeting of GECCAP on 4th June 1979, it was resolved:

126

To wind up the General Election Co-ordinating Committee for Animal Protection on 30th June 1979, and to invite the Joint Consultative Bodies to form an *ad hoc* Consultative Committee which would come into being on 1st July 1979, to keep in close touch with Parliamentary and legislative matters and to bring about a more formal organisation (provisionally to be known as "the National Consultative Committee for Animal Protection") with an agreed constitution to meet regularly, especially whilst Parliament was sitting.

In a memorandum to the joint consultative bodies, Lord Houghton explained the purpose of the new National Consultative Committee:

We must not put the clock back after having experienced the value of consultation and co-operation. The rivalries and inter-society disputes which have done so much harm in the past should now be cast irreversibly into limbo.

At the very least we need an established consultative council where we can all meet together and discuss plans and points of view. While each Society will have its own job to do and its own supporters to listen to and to satisfy, concerted action may get results more quickly than by acting separately.

At the final Meeting of GECCAP on 26th July 1979 the audited accounts of the campaign were approved. The total expenditure amounted to £104,210 (this figure included £50,000 direct expenditure by the RSPCA and further direct expenditure by the LACS of £7,431). The first Meeting of the National Consultative Committee for Animal Protection was held immediately following the final GECCAP meeting, and with the agreement of all the bodies involved the new committee came into being with Lord Houghton as Chairman and David Paterson as Secretary. The campaign to put animals into politics was over. The task facing the joint consultative bodies and the National Consultative Committee for Animal Protection (NCCAP) was now to ensure that animals remained in politics.

PART FOUR

THE FUTURE FOR ANIMALS & ANIMAL WELFARE

CHAPTER XVII

Are we Making Any Progress?

On the 25th July 1979, a joint announcement was made by the Agricultural Departments in Great Britain and the Home Office following a written reply to a question in the House of Commons by Peter Walker, Minister of Agriculture, Fisheries and Food. In this announcement, it was stated that:

> The Government is anxious to increase its impact on matters concerning the welfare of animals. For this purpose we have decided to appoint a Farm Animal Welfare Council which will have the broadest possible remit. [1]

More recently, in November 1979, the Minister gave to the House of Commons further details of the work of the new Council:

> The Council has started to consider its advice on additional legal safeguards to protect farm animals and horses which are being exported and on the way in which the welfare codes for cattle, pigs, domestic fowls and turkeys need to be updated. The Council is free to consider any farm animal welfare matter which falls within its remit and the Government will want its advice on other specific welfare matters from time to time. [2]

The terms of reference for the Council were to keep under review the welfare of farm animals on agricultural land, at markets, and in transit, and to advise the Minister of any legislative or other changes that might be necessary. One area not covered was the slaughter of animals for food. This was particularly important in view of FAWCE's paper on *Pre-Slaughter Stunning Methods and Slaughterhouse Operation in British Abattoirs*. At a meeting between representatives of FAWCE and the Minister in November, we asked that he extend the remit of the Council to include slaughter and on 4th December 1979, the Minister announced that the terms of reference of the Council had been extended to include the welfare of farm animals at the place of slaughter, including handling of animals before slaughter and methods of slaughter.

The joint announcement also referred to animal experimentation, confirming the Government's pledge to bring up to date legislation on experiments on live animals. The Government stated that new legislation would take account of the pending Council of Europe Convention on the protection of laboratory animals, and in the meantime the Home Secretary intended to reconstitute his Advisory Committee on Animal Experiments. The terms of reference would include such matters as may be referred to the Committee by the Secretary of State, including:

(a) specific proposals for experiments on living animals intended to be carried out under authority of the Act;

(b) trends in such experimental work;

(c) questions of policy, procedure or practice;

(d) proposals for revision of the law.

The joint statement by the two responsible ministers was a speedy beginning to implementing the promises made in the Conservative election manifesto. The new Government was elected on 3rd May 1979, and the statement on the setting up of the new committees was made before the end of July.

It was unfortunate, however, that the Government in their anxiety to impress with the speediness of their response, failed to allow time for consultation and as a result ran into difficulties. CRAE, for example, was by no means satisfied with the Home Secretary's proposed composition of the reconstituted Advisory Committee on Animal Experiments, and the Council of the RSPCA refused to allow two of their executive staff members, who had been nominated by the Minister, to serve on the Farm Animal Welfare Council (FAWC).

In both cases the reason was similar; that there was not sufficient welfare representation provided. Indeed, there was not even an attempt at a balance between welfare interests and "animal users." CRAE has made its views very clear to the Home Secretary in writing and in the course of a recent Meeting and it is hoped that when new legislation is introduced, CRAE's views will be taken into account.

132

The RSPCA was in serious difficulty over their decision. A sufficient number of the Society's members disagreed with the decision not to be represented on the Minister's Farm Animal Welfare Council, that the Council of the Society decided to call an extraordinary general meeting of the members which was held at the Central Hall, Westminster on 23rd February 1980. There was a move at the meeting to call for the expulsion of the eleven council members who had voted against representation on FAWC but the three fifths majority required for a motion of no confidence in the Council was not achieved.

On the face of it, this internal dispute within the Society which resulted in considerable unpleasantness and did no good to the animal welfare cause, was about the Society's participation on a Government committee. Whether or not the RSPCA Council took the right decision is a matter for debate, but as the elected representatives of the Society, the right to make that decision was theirs.

However this may be, I personally question the motives of some of those who took issue in this matter. Without doubt there were members who were concerned over the Council's non-acceptance of the Minister's invitation to be represented on FAWC, but how many others saw the possibility of ousting those members of the Council who have been dubbed "left wing extremists?" And how many attended the meeting who had more than a little interest in removing from the Council those with progressive views? In at least one pub in hunting country a notice was posted suggesting: "Miss a day's hunting and attend the RSPCA E.G.M."

Perhaps many of the thousand or so members who attended this meeting and who had genuine reservations about the Council's decision should realise that others voting with them that day may have had far more sinister reasons for casting their vote as they did.

Unfortunately the repercussions from this sad day in the Society's history will continue and no doubt will surface again at the Society's A.G.M. in June.

Returning to the question of animal welfare representation on government committees, it is my view that the die is now cast and for the present at any rate, the Government is not going to lose face by backing down to pressure from the animal welfare lobby. There still remains a strong suspicion in the movement that the

133

Government proposals are merely a cover-up. Much the same was said when the former Labour Government announced their plans for a Council for Animal Welfare and the most common and oft repeated remark I heard at that time was, "Its a whitewash job—they will just talk—nothing will get done and the animals will be no better off."

They may well be right, but we must give it time. The animal welfare movement asked the Government to set up a Standing Royal Commission on Animal Protection. The Labour Government called it a Council for Animal Welfare. The Conservative Goernment have now given us two bodies to be responsible for what are without doubt the worst areas of animal abuse. Both the Farm Animal Welfare Council and the Advisory Committee on Animal Experiments will at least have animal welfare representatives serving on them. It is now up to us to allow the Council and the Advisory Committee to get on with their work—and show us what they can do.

We will know in due course whether the Government really intends to act, or if they are just making the right noises with no intention of bringing about major reforms in the laws governing the welfare of animals. If the latter proves to be the case, I hope the welfare representatives serving on the Advisory Committee or the Farm Animal Welfare Council will immediately resign and publicly state their reasons for doing so. In the meantime we lose nothing in giving the Council and Advisory Committee the opportunity of showing that they have teeth and are prepared to use them.

There have been other recent important and far-reaching developments in the field of animal experimentation. For over a century there has been no change in the legislation governing vivisection. In general, the scientific community have taken the view that the 1876 Act works well, since there have never been any prosecutions under the Act. It was pressure from the animal welfare movement which resulted in the setting up of the Littlewood Enquiry in 1963, an enquiry which in fact achieved very little at the end of the day.

The situation has now dramatically changed due to the work of CRAE and the new climate of public opinion resulting from Animal Welfare Year and the political campaign. The Research Defence Society, through their President, the Earl of Halsbury, has introduced the Laboratory Animals Protection Bill in the House of Lords. Following the Second Reading debate on 25th October 1979, this Bill has been referred to a Select Committee of the House.

Lord Halsbury's Bill is in direct response to the pressure from the animal welfare lobby. As an article in the *New Scientist* observed:

As in 1875, spokesmen for the scientific community wish to take the lead in pushing through new legislation, legislation which will appease the public and defuse the potentially explosive debate while not impeding scientific research.[3]

The Select Committee has taken written and oral evidence and has now entirely redrafted the Bill for return to the House for its further stages. The redrafted Bill, with its provisions for the Home Secretary to make regulations, is now a very different Bill and I believe far more acceptable than the original Halsbury Bill.

Meanwhile in the House of Commons, Mr Peter Fry, Conservative Member for Willingborough, who won fourth place in the ballot for Private Members' Bills, introduced another Bill, after consultation with the RSPCA, titled the Protection of Animals (Scientific Purposes) Bill. In addition, as mentioned earlier, the Council of Europe Convention for the Protection of Laboratory Animals is now nearing its final draft. It is likely therefore that the British Government will want neither of the Private Members' Bills to make progress, but will, I think, use the debates on these Bills and the work of the Select Committee as a sounding board for their own legislation to be introduced later in this Parliament, once the European Convention has been ratified.

CRAE has not been idle during this period of intense activity. Rather than present yet another bill to Parliament, however, CRAE has submitted a memorandum to the Secretary of State and others, outlining what the animal welfare lobby would want to see in any new legislation. As this memorandum says:

CRAE considers that the physiological disturbances associated with the infliction of pain or distress may actually invalidate the results obtained in an experiment. Therefore the principal reform which we wish to see in new legislation is that the infliction of pain or distress shall not be permitted.

The four principal objectives set out in the memorandum are:

1. The restriction of pain;
2. A very substantial reduction in the number of animals used;
3. The development and use of humane alternative methods of research;
4. Public accountability. [4]

There are no easy or quick answers to the vivisection problem. Many people, including myself, want to see the use of live animals in research totally abolished, but the British public and the Government are not yet prepared to go that far. Leaving aside the scientific viewpoint, there is a strong conflict between the welfare of animals on the one hand and fear of disease, injury and death on the other. Nevertheless, public opinion does not assent to much that is now being done under present legislation.

Britain has a great opportunity to take a real lead over this issue. The *New Scientist* article by Dr Judith Hampson referred to above summed up the situation very well:

> Britain now has a unique opportunity to become, once again, the leader in the field of responsible animal protection. We can show Europe the way if we bring into force a good piece of well-thought-out legislation. If we do not do so, a disillusioned animal welfare lobby will no doubt react, as it did in 1875, with a hardening of attitudes. There is, however, one significant difference between 1876 and the present day. The animal welfare lobby is no longer a collection of disorganised animal lovers, it is a unified political force to be reckoned with.

Yet another factor in the vivisection controversy has been the work undertaken by Bill Brown (who sadly died on Christmas Day 1979) and the National Petition for the Protection of Animals. The NPPA petition on animal experimentation has now achieved a staggering total of 1,251,000 signatures which were presented to Parliament before the Second Reading Debate on the Fry Bill on 16th November 1979, and they are still coming in. In addition to collecting signatures for the petition, the supporters of NPPA also gave considerable support to the campaign to "Put Animals Into Politics." Not all societies support the NPPA's petition, on the basis that it does not go far enough in condemning vivisection, but the very number of signatures to the petition provides a significant indication of the strength of public opinion on this issue.

One interesting sidelight to the campaign to "Put Animals Into Politics" was the Charity Commissioners' objection to the RSPCA, as a registered charity, sponsoring advertising for the campaign. The Commissioners considered that an attempt to influence voters in their choice of candidates, to organise supporters in direct political action, and to engage in a political campaign in the way and on the scale envisaged in the advertisement issued by GECCAP was wholly objectionable on the part of a charity. This is another clear example of the difficulties facing registered charities.

As another aside to the recent campaigns, the British Union for the Abolition of Vivisection, the League Against Cruel Sports, the National Anti-Vivisection Society and the Scottish Society for the Prevention of Vivisection decided to hold a formal dinner to honour Lord Houghton, President of Animal Welfare Year, Chairman of the General Election Co-ordinating Committee for Animal Protection, the Committee for the Reform of Animal Experimentation and the National Consultative Committee for Animal Protection. The dinner, attended by representatives of the four societies, was held in the Arts Club in London in July 1979, in appreciation and recognition of Lord Houghton's leadership of the Animal Welfare Movement during these momentous years.

The societies also agreed as a tribute to Lord Houghton to establish an award in his name to be presented annually by each society in turn. At the request of Lord Houghton:

Any member of the Society (in that year responsible for the Award) would be eligible for the Houghton Award, but excluding paid officials or members of Executive Committees or Councils who had in some way given outstanding service to the Society during that year or over a period of years.

The award is to take the form of a badger (the supporters to Lord Houghton's Coat of Arms) modelled in glass, together with a suitably illuminated citation. Of course this tribute can in no way adequately express the debt we all owe Lord Houghton for his leadership and dedication to the cause during recent years.

A further interesting development, which in my view can be attributed only to the growing power and influence of the animal welfare lobby, is the changing attitudes of other bodies concerned with animals. The *British Farmer*, the NFU House magazine, commented:

> It does the industry no good to respond by denouncing all critics as ignorant busybodies, or to argue that things are much worse in other countries, or that faster growth rates, bigger litters, more eggs per bird or improved feed conversion ratios are the final answer to those who contend that there is needless suffering. [5]

It is interesting to note that this editorial included among the critics of modern intensive livestock husbandry, many farmers, and rather more of their wives, and still more of their friends.

The veterinary profession is also becoming much more aware of the growing campaign for animal rights. The British Veterinary Association has set up a Welfare Advisory Group and the Royal College of Veterinary Surgeons has commented on the profession's "clear responsibility for welfare." The President of the Royal College, Mr Nigel Snodgrass, in his address to the Annual General Meeting of the College in June 1979, stated that the College demanded of each new member that he should promise to "make it his constant endeavour to promote the welfare of animals committed to his care." The President also referred to the duty of the College to extend their understanding of those factors which interfered with or imposed limitations on welfare, saying that he was not satisfied that they had discharged this duty with the energy which the public had a right to expect from them. Mr Snodgrass emphasised that the profession had welcomed and encouraged new welfare legislation, but in nearly every case, they had waited until public opinion was already formed, doing little to inspire or guide that opinion.

All these developments I find most encouraging for they quite clearly indicate that there is now a climate of change. I believe that during the next few years, there could well be considerable progress in legislation for the welfare and protection of animals, changes which at the present time may still seem impossible. Such progress depends entirely on the animal welfare movement. The question is, are we strong enough and determined enough to bring about such progress?

CHAPTER XVIII

Public and Private Attitudes

I have already tried to indicate that we are on the verge of great changes in both public and private attitudes towards animals and the rights of animals. Having said that, however, no one should think that the animal rights movement is going to achieve its objectives overnight. Nobody can really believe that whatever legislation results from the present manoeuvering in Parliament, vivisection can be abolished at one stroke. As I have said, the public and indeed Parliament have to resolve the conflict between the welfare and protection of animals from suffering on one hand, and the fear of disease, injury and death of humans on the other.

In the present state of knowledge, there are many animal experiments which the authorities are going to consider essential: basic research into disease, drug screening and testing, public health and diagnostic work and even much substance testing, are likely to continue. Even if government were prepared to act in these areas, they would have to face pressure from inside and outside Parliament from the medical and scientific lobby.

However much we may oppose such research—and I am totally opposed to animal experimentation—this is the situation. The animal welfare societies, particularly the anti-vivisection societies, therefore have two options open to them. They either say that neither of the Private Members' Bills, nor pending European proposals, nor the Government's own Bill when it comes, will satisfy them because there is no ban on all, or at least some experiments, or the societies can adopt a more positive approach to new legislation. By a positive approach, I mean proposing amendments to the Bills now before Parliament which will strengthen the law as far as is possible to prevent the causing to animals of pain or distress. In other words the objective is to get the best deal for laboratory animals that we possibly can. In my view, this is extremely important. Although the Private Members' Bills are unlikely to make progress, the Government will without a doubt draft their own legislation on what comes out of these Bills—from the Select Committee in the House of Lords on the Halsbury Bill and from the Standing Committee in the Commons on the Fry Bill.

The easy option for the societies is to follow the first course. If new legislation is condemned because it does not go far enough, the societies can stand back and tell their members, "There you are—the Government has sold us down the river. There is little or no improvement in the lot of laboratory animals in the new Act." To adopt this position and to refuse to comment on impending legislation, other than to say, "We do not want it," would be burying one's head in the sand. The legislation will not go away merely because the societies do not want it, and the end result would be that the scientists would get the kind of legislation they want, which may last for another hundred years.

The second option is much more difficult and open to criticism, but in my view it is the right one. Whatever the animal welfare organisations say, new legislation will almost certainly be placed on the statute book during the life of this Parliament. Therefore to comment as strongly as possible, to gain as many safeguards by putting down amendments to the Bills as they pass through committee, is achieving all that is possible at this time. CRAE has already stated its position in the memorandum, *Proposals for Change in the Legislation Governing the Use of Live Animals in Research, Experiments and other Laboratory Purposes*, and has also given written and oral evidence to the Select Committee based on this memorandum.

It was the animal welfare societies through the campaign to "Put Animals Into Politics," which were responsible for setting in motion the proposals for new legislation now before Parliament and that process is gathering momentum. We have to face the consequences of our own success. Never before has there been so much parliamentary activity on animal welfare, with two comprehensive and well thought out Bills on animal experimentation before both Houses of Parliament. The party system is a process of reform and not of revolution. Great and dramatic changes are rarely brought about by a single measure and the ideal in the minds of the reformers is frequently the

142

unattainable in the short term. Public opinion is the impetus for and parliamentary action is the instrument of change.

The present position entails all the problems and dilemmas which have faced reformers throughout the history of progress. As Lord Houghton has said, "Those who refuse to help erect the milestones are not on the march."

I have concentrated these comments on the vivisection debate since it is the one I know best, but similar argument applies to all other fields of animal exploitation, factory farming, domestic pets, horses, live exports of food animals, hunting, and all the many other issues which concern us and which will respond to change and reform only as the concept of animal rights gains ground. New legislation now is but one battle in a long war, a war which none of us living today will see the final victory, but eventual victory there will be for the rights of animals.

One of the major issues in the CRAE memorandum which may not sound very exciting is our insistence on enabling clauses in any new legislation. Enabling clauses mean exactly what they say and permit the responsible minister as and when he deems necessary, to introduce further changes or restrictions by means of regulations or orders laid before Parliament under the Act, without having to bring in new or amending legislation.

As stated in the CRAE Memorandum:

We appreciate that not all the recommendations contained in this Memorandum may be acceptable to the Secretary of State and the Government at this point in time, but we urge the Government to come as close to our proposals as possible when framing new legislation and *to allow scope in any new legislation for the progressive tightening up of restrictions on the use of living animals.*

This will give all the animal welfare societies the opportunity of continuing to press the government of the day to act for the further protection of animals used for research or in other fields, as further knowledge is gained, for example, in the use of alternatives to animals or when new abuses or excesses come to light. This will be the next battle.

There are many people working in the field of animal welfare who will not be prepared to accept this view. They will argue, quite

143

rightly, that this is compromise and in no way will they be prepared to accept anything less than total abolition of vivisection or the banning of all factory farming methods. No one wants to see the end of such practices more than I. Like many others and in spite of many years working professionally in animal welfare, I still suffer with the animals when I read and see what man is capable of doing to them in the name of progress. But to ask for an end to all this in the world as it is, is crying for the moon. If, during my lifetime, we can achieve some relief from the pain, distress and misery endured by so many animals, then I believe that the first battle is not lost.

There are so many areas where we can win. As stated in an editorial in the *Cambridge News* on the recent publicity over experiments at the Animal Physiology Unit at Babraham, Cambridge:

> There is a point at which one ought to admit that animals do have a basic dignity and that however important some experiments are we accept that they trespass upon their right to that dignity to an unacceptable degree. [1]

An eminent pathologist, Professor G. Scott of the Royal Free Hospital, speaking at the British Veterinary Association Congress in Aberdeen in 1979, is reported as claiming that "too often extreme and unrealistic experiments are being carried out on animals." [2] Earlier in this book, I referred to experiments conducted in Edinburgh into "the effects of Breed, Birthcoat and Bodyweight on the Cold Resistence of Newborn Lambs" and now writing this chapter some time later, I can report that the Agricultural Research Council have stopped any further experiments into the effect of cold on sheep. In a statement to the press, the Agricultural Research Council denied that the test had been stopped because of pressure from animal welfare groups, stating:

> We have learned a lot from the project and we are satisfied that the experiments would be useful in the future in breeding programmes to produce hardier lambs. [3]

It does not matter that the ARC deny the reason for stopping this work, the experiments have been stopped and that is what matters.

On the subject of experimentation, let me quote just a few examples taken at random, from the many reports in my office. All these experiments were conducted in British laboratories during the past two years.

Young kittens subjected to surgery to remove muscles and tissues from the eyes and total removal of the nicitating membrane. After recovery the kittens were trained to lick a fish reward whilst viewing a scene which was to represent a safe stimulus and to stop licking if a dangerous stimulus was presented. Failure to respond resulted in the animals being given an electric shock. (*Journal of Experimental Brain Research* (1979)34)

The Sciatic nerves and saphaneous nerves of rats and mice were exposed and dissected by surgery under ether anaesthetic. The skin was then sewn up. Complete deadness of the foot occurred and there was severe autotomy (biting of their own limbs). 85% of the animals had severely bitten limbs after five weeks and it was concluded that the animals bit themselves due to adverse nerve sensations in the limbs after induced nerve damage. (*Pain* Vol. 6 No. 2 1979)

In the search for male anti-fertility drugs, a compound was tested for tocixity on 24 young adult male rhesus monkeys. In a series of experiments of differing dosages and time scales the drug was tested. To quote from one test: "Administration over one month": "Both monkeys dosed at 500mg/kg—day had to be killed *in extremis* within the first week. They had vomited on several occasions, usually during the night. The animals became inactive and were frequently found to be recumbent; they also lost weight". (*Toxicology* 9 (1978) 219-225)

Many experiments such as these could be prevented now and that would be a battle won.

In West Germany, a court has ruled that the battery system, *per se* is cruel since the cages deprive hens of the ability to follow instinctive behaviour, such as scratching, stretching, flapping their wings, and preening. There is now hope that we might see an end to this method of producing eggs, which is disliked by all (except the producers). The battery system becomes even less acceptable when one reads a report in the *Scotsman* that the Chairman of the National Farmers' Union Poultry Committee has called for the killing off of two and a half million egg-laying chickens in order to solve the poultry industry's over-production crisis.[4]

Conditions in British slaughterhouses, particularly with regard to humane pre-slaughter stunning, is another area where much progress can and will be made. Close tethering of breeding sows is also an example of where animal welfare societies can win. There are many others. Indeed, there are so many battles to win.

I have made this statement because I believe that without determined effort and continued unity of purpose, we shall not even achieve this much progress. I have emphasised throughout this book the necessity, above all else, for joint action. Indeed this was the main purpose in writing the book. I have tried to show the results of such joint action; for the first time in the history of the British Parliament, the major parties had something to say about animal welfare in the election manifestos; CRAE as a joint body, is able to have direct contact with the Home Secretary and the senior members of his department; likewise FAWCE has established direct links with the Minister and the Ministry, something which no individual animal welfare organisation could achieve; the press and the media now continually publish articles and programmes on animal exploitation—all this in a mere four years. In a review of 1979 the *Veterinary Record* commented:

> More generally the topic of animal welfare was rarely out of the headlines. For the first time, it was brought into the political arena with debates in Parliament and both major parties emphasising their commitment to the welfare causes.[5]

What have we achieved in the past hundred years working on our own? We are now making some progress—are we going to throw it all away by going our own separate ways?

It is necessary to say this and I say it with real sadness, because already there are signs that some organisations want to return to ploughing their own lonely furrow. The seeds of disunity are buried deeply in history, and in spite of two national campaigns, where a large number of organisations have co-operated to achieve common aims and specific results, suspicion and hostility still remain just below the surface.

The RSPCA is the largest animal welfare organisation in the world and it is my view that some of the causes of disunity stem from the composition of the RSPCA and its acceptance over the years of the conventional standards of the day (e.g. until 1976, the Society would not condemn hunting), coupled with its emphasis on charitable work. This indeed has been the main pre-occupation of the Society from its inception, and in common with many Victorian charities it has worked for the alleviation and prevention of cruelty, but has not challenged, until recently, the vested interests which perpetrate the real cruelties to animals in the name of our affluent consumer society.

This has inevitably led to the formation of smaller independent, specialist societies, which are frequently very active and extremely vocal. The RSPCA is a lumbering giant which resents being jockeyed along by the smaller campaigning and often non-charitable bodies. By the same token, the smaller organisations do not like being beholden to and taking second place to big brother. The animal societies have been the last to recognise the need for co-operation and collective action largely, I believe, on account of any counter-balance to the size, influence and affluence of the RSPCA.

However in the world outside, super-powers like the USA do not remain outside NATO, or the USSR outside the Warsaw Pact; they lead from inside, building allies from friendly smaller powers. The belief of the RSPCA as a super-power and for that matter the belief of the smaller campaigning organisations that they do not need allies, is an ever present threat to future unity and progress.

The present position of the RSPCA with regard to continuing joint action is somewhat unclear. Although nominally a member of all the joint consultative bodies, their representatives rarely attend meetings and the Society now services none of these bodies. (Originally the RSPCA provided secretarial services for CRAE, FAWCE and HEC). As the largest organisation in the world, the Society should be leading these joint bodies with expert advice and servicing both of which are available from the large staff at Horsham.

Tribute must be paid however to Richard D. Ryder, the immediate past Chairman of the RSPCA Council, for all the support he gave to the concept of unity during his two year tenure of office. Not only did he give the fullest support to "Animal Welfare Year" and the campaign to "Put Animals Into Politics," but he also achieved a great deal during his two short years in office to make the RSPCA an active society, in areas other than those traditionally the work of the organisation, namely the care and welfare of pet animals. In his final address as Chairman to the Annual General Meeting of the Society in June 1979, Richard Ryder referred to the formation of the RSPCA and the early campaigning spirit of its founders. He continued: "I would submit that the wheel has now turned full circle and the RSPCA once again has begun to become a crusading enterprise."[6] I hope that before too much time has elapsed this great organisation will realise that working in unity with smaller societies is to the benefit of all—particularly the animals.

The National Anti-Vivisection Society is another organisation which has turned its back on joint action. The NAVS did not support Animal Welfare Year and I was therefore more than pleased when the Society gave their wholehearted support to the political campaign. The branches of the NAVS, together with their Assistant General Secretary, Brian Gunn, were some of the most active groups in the campaign.

Early in 1980, the NAVS advised that they had decided not to give further support to CRAE because in their view the proposals so far recommended by CRAE were of such a weak nature that, even were they to be accepted by this or some future government, they would have little or no benefit to laboratory animals. Anyone who has studied CRAE's Proposals for change in legislation could hardly say the recommendations are in any way weak or would not prevent considerable suffering of laboratory animals.

What then is the attitude of the grass roots members of the societies to co-operation and unity? If the mail received during the election campaign is anything to go by, they want to see the national societies working together. Here are some excerpts from letters sent to us:

As members of the BUAV, NAVS, RSPCA, UFAW, SSPV and various other small groups, may we express our opinion that we would very much like to see the continuation of GECCAP. It can only go to serve good by being united and we think it has been an excellent and worthwhile campaign.

- London -

I believe that your objective in bringing all the organisations concerned with animal welfare together is an excellent idea and

148

Protest march in Oxford organised by the Action Group "Animal Aid", October, 1979. (*Photograph by courtesy of "Oxford Mail & Times"*).

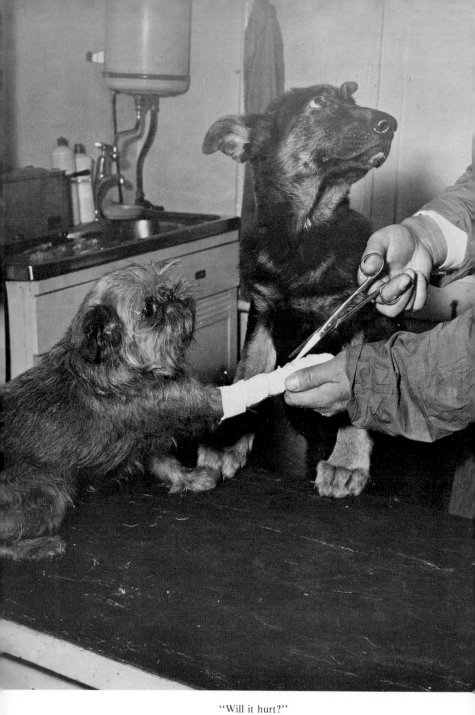

"Will it hurt?"

The Houghton/Platt Memorandum.
Members of the Houghton Group outside the Home Office:
Left to right:
The Author—Clive Hollands, the late Lord Platt, Dr. Kit Pedler,
Wm. Jordan, Lord Houghton and Richard D. Ryder.

The Author and Chairman of Animal Welfare Year greets T.V. personality, Johnny Morris at an Event organised by the Surrey and Hampshire A.W.Y. group. Also in the picture, Mrs Chapman, Secretary of the Group, Richard D. Ryder, Dr. Gordon Latto, Mr. David Paterson, and Miss Anne Douglass, Chairman of the group.
(Photograph by courtesy of J. Malecki, A.R.P.S.)

Labour Party Conference, Blackpool. Campaign advertising outside the Information Centre.

one which is necessary if the case for a more comprehensive approach to animal protection is to be achieved.

- Coventry -

The problem in the past, of course, has been there was no central co-ordination point such as the one you have now founded. Please keep up your publicity campaign.

- Arabian Gulf -

It is high time all the animal welfare groups got together in a unified force.

- St. Andrews -

I am delighted to know that the societies I support have joined hands to stop the horrible cruelties.

- Robertsbridge -

What you said about the need for unity was, I think, the most important thing said at the recent meeting of the Anglican Society for the Welfare of Animals.

- Southampton -

I sometimes wonder just how far out of touch are executive committees and headquarters staff of some animal welfare societies with their own membership. Almost without exception, the many thousands of people I met, or who wrote to me during Animal Welfare Year and the campaign to "Put Animals Into Politics," were overjoyed and surprised to learn that the societies were at long last working together. The opposition were not only surprised, they were dismayed and alarmed. As the *Field* observed:

Most animal welfare groups use lawful means to further their ends and strive to win support in Parliament for their aims. They pursue notoriously separate paths however. Several groups with similar aims may campaign quite separately and dissipate the strength of the welfare movement.

A determined and professional effort has now been made to unite them all behind the slogan Putting Animals Into Politics. [7]

I am firmly convinced that there is desperate need for unity in the animal welfare movement. I will accept, however, that there are problems involved in working together. I referred to the need for unity and the difficulties involved in the paper I presented at the

149

Animal Rights Symposium at Trinity College, Cambridge in
August 1977, when I said:

> At a time when commercial organisations spend vast sums of
> money on promoting products, and when highly organised
> pressure groups like the trade unions and the student bodies can
> call upon their enormous manpower resources to exert pressure
> on public opinion and for political lobbying, the animal welfare
> movement must come to terms with the fact that it is only by
> joint effort that it can really succeed. It is therefore essential that
> a spirit of co-operation between organisations should be
> encouraged and, even at some cost to themselves, societies must
> be prepared to sink their differences in order to work together to
> ensure that real protection is given to animals. [8]

To achieve such unity of purpose it is necessary for the societies
to resolve their differences and even to surrender a little of their
sovereignty. There will be times when a society's view or proposal
will not be acceptable to the majority of the other groups serving on
a joint consultative body, or where a particular organisation is
criticised by others for action it has taken. In this event, that society
must be sensible enough to bow to the will of the majority for the
greater good and not pack their bags and leave.

The ordinary men, women and indeed children who give us, the
animal welfare societies, their support, want to see us working
together. Of that I am certain. If we can achieve what has been
achieved in the past four years, what can we hope for in the future?

CHAPTER XIX

Compassion is the Bugler

Where does the animal welfare movement go from here? Are we going to recognise that far more unites us than divides us, or are we going to revert to being lone voices crying in the wilderness? It is impossible to tell what will happen, but I should like to conclude by expressing some of my own thoughts on what the future may hold and what I see as the path forward.

I think that the joint consultative bodies (CCC, CRAE, FAWCE, HEC and NJEWC), backed by the National Consultative Committee for Animal Protection, will continue to develop and grow in effectiveness. If I am correct in this assumption, I see these bodies being accepted, especially in Parliament, as the authoritative and responsible voice of the animal welfare movement. Societies which insist on remaining outside these bodies will remove themselves from the main stream of thought, and as a direct result, will become gradually more isolated and eventually will have little or no voice in the debate. It is my hope that all animal welfare organisations will give long and serious thought to the future and to the attitude of their own society to the new and exciting developments of the past few years.

Surely, to everyone who has ever loved an animal, to all of us who serve in this great movement, compassion is the bugler and our rallying point. We seek to establish the rights of animals, and although there may be many different pathways to this goal, the bugler's call to arms is still the same and is based on compassion. I am not interested to know whether a society is too moderate, too extreme or even too militant. There is room in the movement for all of us; we are all needed and our eventual goal is the same.

There are many problems which beset this movement, not least of which stem from pettiness, jealousy, bitterness and the desire to go one better than the next even to the extent of battling among ourselves. None of these is worthy of the great movement we represent. I sometimes think that in our efforts to become the organisation with the most members, or with our name most frequently mentioned in the press we forget the reality of the pain and misery suffered by so many animals. Such things do not matter, so long as what .we all stand for is placed continuously before the public, press and Parliament. A South African author, Stuart Cloete brings home the sometimes forgotten anguish of the creatures in *The Curve and the Tusk* with this symbolic reference to ivory piano keys:

> The maiden crying over her music lesson is only the last echo of a scream of an elephant dying in Africa that had reached across the world . . . for ivory is born of pain, horror and crime. . . . The agony of the hanging ivory Jesus on a miniature wooden cross and that of the elephant who died that it could be made, are related.[1]

Maybe we should all try a little harder to see beyond the obvious and the accepted side of our work to what lies beneath.

Assuming that I am right in my vision of a strong and unified animal welfare movement of the future, the onus is then placed squarely on the shoulders of the Government for action. The Government must now act in a responsible manner to discharge the promises made to the animal welfare lobby. Legislation must offer real protection and safeguards for the welfare of animals. The price of implementing such legislation will on occasion take the form of loss of commercial profit or of higher prices. Even so, this, and future governments, must be bold and fearless in demonstrating that the rights of animals (and not weak and unenforceable regulations) will form the basis for legislation. If they do not, the signs are already there, as Lord Houghton has warned:

> There can be no doubt that the time for animals has arrived—the younger and more militant members of animal welfare are waiting patiently to see what GECCAP can do to persuade Government to act. The patience of the young is often short-lived and for many of them the wheels of Parliament grind slowly—too slowly.[2]

Mr Jeff Rooker, M.P., in the debate in the Commons in March 1979, said much the same thing:

152

It is a new look animal welfare which has been motivated by the previous inaction and an influx of younger people who do not have the patience of the older generation. If they see no action forthcoming they will be forced, and happy, to take direct action.[3]

I am afraid that if the Government are not seen to take these issues seriously or if attempts are made merely to make the right noises to placate the animal lobby, I see no alternative for the future other than growing direct and more militant action by the young now in the animal welfare movement. There is no question in my mind of condemning or defending such action. Whatever the animal welfare societies say, the activists will go their own way and, rightly or wrongly, this is already beginning to happen.

The first of the organised groups to take direct action, although legal direct action, was the Hunt Saboteurs Assocation. This organisation was founded to disrupt hunting of animals with hounds. In spite of its bad press, the HSA members are often more sinned against than sinning. Members have suffered badly over the years from the actions of the hunt 'heavies.'

In 1973, the Band of Mercy came into being and into the headlines with acts of violence against the property and vehicles of vivisection laboratories and others. This group ended with what became known as the trial of the "Oxford Three." Since that time a number of activist groups have come into being, the majority, like Animal Aid, being concerned with legal direct action only. Animal Aid has over the past few years been most successful in organising mass demonstrations and marches and, in so doing, has gained considerable support and membership.

CAW (Co-ordinating Animal Welfare) is yet another new group of young enthusiasts, who are determined to see that the animal welfare movement becomes more effective. Many of these groups still have much to learn about the use of diplomacy and tactics rather than sheer brute force, to gain their objectives, but their determination is a sign of the times. The Animal Liberation Front, the ALF as it is known, has taken the law into its own hands and its members frequently spend much of their time in prison cells. In 1976-77 alone it has been estimated that the ALF caused over three hundred thousand pounds worth of damage to laboratories and factory farms.[4]

153

Yet another indication of this mood has been the publication in recent years of books advocating militant and violent action. I remember many years ago when I first came into animal welfare, finding a copy of a privately printed book in a plain cover, entitled *The Clansmen*. I cannot now find the book or remember who was the author, but it was a fantasy of destruction and death to all those who exploited animals for their own gain, whether in laboratories, factory farms or on the hunting field.

Much more recently, *I want to go to Moscow*, by Maureen Duffy, is the story of dedicated and extraordinary men and women, determined to abolish cruelty to animals by any means necessary, including the use of high explosives. One of the characters outlines to a newcomer the size of the problem:

> No doubt you know that the whole animal welfare movement is quite big. It's divided into lots of societies each with its own particular sphere of activity. Each group thinks its own horror is the worst and works to end it. Put them all together and you have a total picture of exploitation and death that can only be ended by complete change of attitude and legislation; not only here but all over the world. [5]

Another such book is *Leviathan*, by John Gordon Davis. This is a story of a battle against the whalers, with no holds barred, as the conservationists attack the whaling ships with gun and bomb. Real life has now overtaken fiction as during the past year whaling ships have been attacked and sunk by protesters. In July 1979 the conservation vessel *Sea Shepherd* rammed the whaler *Sierra* holing her above the waterline. The *Sierra* was repaired but later sunk in Lisbon harbour probably with limpet mines. Two other whaling vessels were sunk in April 1980 at a Spanish port and again limpet mines were thought to have been used. The final sentence of *Leviathan* is a chilling reminder of what man is capable of doing to these magnificent creatures.

> the blue whale calf swam, calling, calling, but he did not hear any answers, and it was probable that he never would, because there were so few blue whales left in all the oceans, and there were many millions of cubic miles between them, and all the time his heart was crying out. . . . [6]

The Beagle Brigade by Innes Hamilton is a novel also dealing with direct action, but action in a more gentlemanly and "English" manner, but nevertheless action which involves the deliberate breaking of the law in order to influence a government.[7]

So where do we go from here? The supreme task before us is to continue to mobilise public opinion to the point of causing concern in the political arena. In this, we have to pursue further the astonishing success achieved during the campaign to "Put Animals Into Politics." The political parties must feel that the animal welfare lobby is to be reckoned with, both inside the parties and electorally among a large number of uncommitted voters who have a concern for animal welfare. This, I believe, must be achieved during the life of this Parliament.

How do we go about it? Firstly, let us see a strong and united animal welfare movement, seeking reform in a realistic rather than an idealistic manner, while not losing sight of our final objective which is to ensure that, in the words of the Universal Declaration of the Rights of Animals, "all animals are born with an equal claim on life and the same rights to existence."

Let us break down the attitudes towards "inferiority" which have plagued human relationships throughout the ages ("the natives"; "class distinction"; "conquest"; "enslavement") and challenge both the high gods of consumerism and commercialism and the supremacy of the law of supply and demand. Let us be freedom fighters in the battle for animal rights, which is, and must be, a political fight and not merely the undertaking of charitable work to alleviate the unjust suffering of the few. One thing is certain: we shall never have another opportunity as we have now. We cannot afford to lose the momentum built up over the last few years, and every animal welfare organisation in this country, charitable or otherwise, should immediately embark on a sustained and co-ordinated programme of publicity to the very limit of available funds. Each society can develop its own programme, but the total effort must be co-ordinated for maximum effect.

Such activity, in addition to paid advertising, should include an attempt to influence radio, television and the press for still more programmes, articles and features on different areas of animal exploitation; pressure on government ministers and their departments by the use of letters and questions tabled in both

Houses of Parliament; frequent and personal contact with M.P.'s in their constituencies and at the House; more demonstrations to direct public attention to legalised cruelties; involvement of young people everywhere, and particularly in schools and universities; and the setting up of an Animal Protection Action Fund as a political fund for the movement which is so often hamstrung by its charitable status. Perhaps charitable societies should even seriously consider the implications of their status as charities, financially and also within the public, political and parliamentary struggle to lift animal welfare into the sphere of the ethics of human (and humane) behaviour.

Finally, let us see the British public responding by giving their unqualified support to reasonable and responsible demands being made for reform, and in turn let us see the Government responding to those demands. Let us see Great Britain taking this "unique opportunity to become, once again, the leader in the field of responsible animal protection."

For all of us, let compassion be the bugler. . . .

ROYAL SOCIETY FOR THE PREVENTION OF CRUELTY TO ANIMALS

The Manor House, Horsham, Sussex RH12 1HG.

THE ST. ANDREW ANIMAL FUND LTD.

10 Queensferry Street, Edinburgh EH2 4PG.

ANIMAL WELFARE YEAR, 1976

The Royal Society for the Prevention of Cruelty to Animals and the St. Andrew Animal Fund jointly announce the proposal to designate 1976 as "Animal Welfare Year".

This proposal was first made at a Conference of Scottish Animal Welfare Societies by Mr. F. A. Burden, M.P., Chairman of the Animal Welfare Group in the House of Commons, as 1976 is the Centenary of *The Cruelty to Animals Act,* the oldest Animal Welfare legislation now on the Statute Book.

The R.S.P.C.A, and the St. Andrew Animal Fund have agreed that, to be successful, "Animal Welfare Year" would require the active support and financial backing of the majority of Animal Welfare Societies in Gt. Britain. It is hoped that the Societies to whom this Memorandum is addressed, will seize this opportunity to advance the work of the whole Animal Welfare Movement in Gt. Britain.

In the preliminary discussions, suggestions have been put forward regarding the scope of Animal Welfare Year and methods which could be employed to implement the proposal. These suggestions are summarised below to provide a basis for further discussion.

AIMS OF ANIMAL WELFARE YEAR

Although *The Cruelty to Animals Act, 1876* legislates on experiments on animals, it is felt that the scope of Animal Welfare Year should be on a much broader front, the emphasis being on the Centenary of the oldest Animal Welfare Legislation on the Statute Book. Four of the five headings suggested by Miss Janet Fookes, M.P. in her Motion on Animal Welfare debated in the House of Commons on 14th December, 1973, are felt to be appropriate.

Pet Animals
Laboratory Animals
Farm Animals
The Transit of Animals

in other words, animals "handled by" or "controlled by" man. "Animals" being domestic animals as defined in *The Protection of Animals Act 1911* Section 15(a)—(d) and *The Protection of Animals (Scotland) Act, 1912* Section 13(a)—(d).

In the present worrying financial situation facing all charities, "Animal Welfare Year" could well be the means of focusing public attention on the work of Animal Welfare Societies and of enlisting fresh support.

The aims of "Animal Welfare Year" are threefold:
1. To bring to the public's attention the considerable progress in Animal Welfare Legislation which has taken place during the past hundred years.
2. To focus public attention on the present areas of concern and the likely developments in animal exploitation during the next hundred years unless adequate legislation is enacted.
3. The final aim is, of course, to arouse sufficient public interest and concern during 1976, so that sympathetic Members of Parliament could use such support in the future to urge Government action to revise and bring up-to-date present legislation, and for the introduction of new legislation—**Where the Emphasis must be on the Protection and Wellbeing of Animals and not on Commercial Interest or Profit.**

158

METHODS—FUND-RAISING AND PUBLICITY

It is envisaged that throughout the year, events would be organised by individual Societies at headquarters and branch levels to raise funds and gain publicity for "Animal Welfare Year". In addition, the Organising Committee would arrange National Events designed to focus attention on "Animal Welfare Year" and to raise funds for further publicity. Obviously, as much use as possible would be made of the mass media, including special programmes on Television and Radio.

FIRST STEPS

(A) It is hoped that all Societies receiving this Memorandum will discuss the proposal in the light of their own particular work, and will decide if they are prepared to support "Animal Welfare Year":

    (i)   By taking an active part.

    (ii) By providing direct financial support and

    (iii) If required, by nominating an Official to serve on the Organising Committee.

(B) A One Day Exploratory Conference will be held in the Dundee Room, Kenilworth Hotel, Great Russell Street, London WC1B 3LB, 10 a.m. to 4 p.m. on Friday 14th February 1975, to which all Societies receiving this Memorandum are invited to send one delegate to discuss the proposals for "Animal Welfare Year". At this Conference a final decision will be taken, depending upon the volume of support, both active and financial, indicated by the delegates as to whether the proposal should be adopted.

(C) In the event that the proposal is adopted, the Conference will then elect an Organising Committee of approximately twenty Members which will represent a cross-section of the Animal Welfare interests involved.

(D) The Organising Committee will advertise for, and appoint, a salaried Organiser; (the salary of the Organiser up to certain limits has already been guaranteed by the St. Andrew Animal Fund).

159

(E) It is hoped that office accommodation and secretarial assistance will be available in Central London for the Organiser whose first duties will be to apply to the Charity Commissioners for registration as a "Charity" and the opening of a Special Account in the name of the "Animal Welfare Year Fund".

It is hoped that the foregoing will provide the Committees of individual Societies with sufficient information to discuss this proposal in depth. It is emphasised that these are only first thoughts, and it is hoped that all Societies taking part will produce their own ideas and more detailed proposals for implementing "Animal Welfare Year".

IF GIVEN SUFFICIENT SUPPORT, "ANIMAL WELFARE YEAR" COULD BE THE MAJOR ANIMAL PROTECTION EVENT OF THE CENTURY—IF NOT OF ALL TIME, AND RESULTS COULD BE MORE FAR-REACHING THAN MIGHT BE IMAGINED. THERE CAN BE NO DOUBT THAT THE ATTITUDE IN PARLIAMENT IS READY FOR A MAJOR REFORM OF ANIMAL WELFARE LEGISLATION AND IT SHOULD NOT BE FORGOTTEN THAT THE ECHOES FROM "ANIMAL WELFARE YEAR" IN GREAT BRITAIN COULD WELL TRAVEL ROUND THE WORLD.

Finally, it is requested that all Societies wishing to be represented at the Conference to discuss "Animal Welfare Year" on 14th February, 1975, should forward the name and appointment of the delegate to:

The Secretary,
St. Andrew Animal Fund,
10 Queensferry Street
Edinburgh, EH2 4PG.
Telephone: 031-225 6039

not later than 15th January 1975. There will be no fee for attending the Conference, but delegates will have to make their own travelling arrangements and accommodation etc., if required.

Major R. F. Seager,
Executive Director,
Royal Society for the Prevention of Cruelty to Animals

Clive Hollands
Secretary, St. Andrew Animal Fund.

Edinburgh, 10th December, 1974.

ANIMAL WELFARE YEAR
PARTICIPATING SOCIETIES

Albrighton Animal Rescue Team
Anglican Society for Animal Welfare
Anglo-Italian Society for the Protection of Animals
Anglo-Spanish Animal Welfare Society
Animal Life Brigade
Animal Welfare Trust
Barnes Wildlife and Animal Welfare Group
Beauty Without Cruelty (International)
Beauty Without Cruelty (Scotland)
Bleakholt Animal Sanctuary
Blue Cross
Bransby Home of Rest for Horses
British Horse Society
British Union for the Abolition of Vivisection
Brooke Hospital for Animals, Cairo
Captive Animals Protection Society
Catholic Study Circle for Animal Welfare
Cats Protection League
Central Council for SPCA's in Scotland
Central Dog Registry
Compassion in World Farming
Conference of Animal Welfare Societies
Crusade Against All Cruelty to Animals
Dog Aid Society of Scotland
Dogs Home, Battersea
Dr. Hadwen Trust
Edinburgh Cat Protection League
Edinburgh Dog and Cat Home
Farnham & Aldershot Animal Rescue Service
Fellowship of Life
Friends' Animal Welfare and Anti-Vivisection Society
Friends of Animals League

Fund for the Replacement of Animals in Medical Experiments
Heswall and District Animal Welfare Society
Horses & Ponies Protection Society
Humane Education Society
Humane Research Trust
International League for the Protection of Horses
International Society for the Protection of Animals
Japan Animal Welfare Society
Lawson Tait Medical and Scientific Research Trust
League Against Cruel Sports
Movement Against Cruel Experiments
National Canine Defence League
National Council for Animals Welfare
National Dog Rescue Co-ordinating Committee
National Society for the Abolition of Cruel Sports
Northern Counties Horse Protection Society
Peoples Dispensary for Sick Animals
Performing Animals Defence League
Ponies of Britain
Protect Our Livestock Group
Royal Society for the Prevention of Cruelty to Animals
Scottish Anti-Vivisection Society
Scottish Society for the Prevention of Vivisection
Scottish Wildlife Trust
Sidmouth Animal Welfare Group
Society for Animal Welfare in Israel
St. Andrew Animal Fund
Tailwaggers Club Trust
Tayside Cat Fund
Ulster Society for the Prevention of Cruelty to Animals (Inc.)
Welfare of Animals Committee (National Council of Women)
Whitley Animal Protection Trust
Wood Green Animal Shelter
Worcester Animal Protection Association
World Federation for the Protection of Animals (British Committee)

The concept of Animal Welfare Year is inspired by a challenge to the selfish creed of the rights of man to the exclusion of all others. It is a recognition of the claims of all living things to their place in the continuing evolution of the inhabitants of the earth.

The aim of animal welfare used to be largely the exposure and punishment of individual acts of cruelty or of 'causing unnecessary suffering' inflicted by acts of violence or culpable neglect. In more recent times animal husbandry has turned to intensive methods, and the use of living animals for laboratory purposes has increased. These, together with the relentless pressures of population growth and the spread of lethal pollution bring a new dimension to the moral and ecological issues involved. Although wanton cruelty by wicked or thoughtless people is still prevalent and is an offence against the law, the new threat to standards of animal welfare comes from the organised pursuit of social, commercial or economic objectives, desirable in themselves, which take all enjoyment out of life for millions of birds and animals.

There are double standards in most of our thinking about animal welfare. There is, for example, much more concern about cruelty to pets than to pigs. Horses and dogs are given greater protection from ill-treatment than donkeys and cats. We tend to distinguish between animals for pleasure and animals for food, and accept lower standards of welfare for those whose lives are brutish and short. What is more, there are some things we would rather not know, and which we are discouraged from even getting to know.

The pet owner cannot be entirely absolved from his part in the great national hypocrisy about our love of animals. I need not dwell upon the fate of the abandoned dog or cat and the heartless rejection of an animal formerly given shelter and affection. The depressing toll of destruction of unwanted pets and the distasteful burden thrust upon voluntary bodies whose work is to promote animal welfare is deplorably heavy.

A fresh and courageous spirit prompts this great effort of three-score voluntary organisations to make life more tolerable for animals we know, and to safeguard the very existence of species threatened with ruthless exploitation and extinction. In no sphere is the greed and callousness of man more reprehensible than in the forest, the jungle and the sea.

Animal Welfare Year calls for human understanding of the full meaning of life, and the beauties and mysteries of Creation. It is an outrage against nature to think that after millions of years this wonderful world is solely the property of man who denies all rights to species other than his own.

Houghton of Sowerby

Extract from the Report 'Church and Nation'
to The General Assembly of the Church of Scotland, 1978

The General Assembly of 1977, briefly noting Animal Welfare Year, commended the welfare of animals to the consideration of all citizens and urged that no experiments be carried out on living animals unless vitally necessary to human or animal welfare.

Since certain developments have taken place subsequently and because of the general interest in animal welfare, both on humanitarian and environmental grounds, it is felt timely to give further consideration to this topic.

The Christian Approach

The theological ground for a Christian approach to animal welfare is in the Biblical doctrine of Creation. The unity of creation is affirmed as a corallary of the Oneness of God. Man is one with all things animate and inanimate being composed of the same elements "dust of the earth", but he has been given also a unique character and role in the scheme of things in that he bears the image of God and has been given a delegated permission to exercise authority over the creation including the animals. That all seems simple and ideal, but the Bible makes clear that a complicating and perverse state of affairs overlies this basic pattern the essence of which is a fouling-up of relationships. Man, left to his own devices, is inclined to get his relationships wrong, whether it be in regard to God, his fellow-man or his fellow-creatures. In his relationship to the animals man misuses his authority in the direction of exploitation and cruelty. Nevertheless he regains his true relationship as a responsible steward of the creation to the degree that he becomes "renowned in his mind" in regard to that particular relationship. (Romans 12:2.)

Humane concern in the matter of animals must therefore be welcomed and fostered by the Church but this is not to go all the way with the sentimentality which sometimes becomes associated with this subject. A balance has to be kept between economic reality and ethical idealism. A case in point arises in connection with modern farming techniques.

Farm Animals

As a result of widespread public disquiet at some of the excesses of intensive animal husbandry and following the publication of Ruth Harrison's book *Animal Machines* in 1964, the Minister of Agriculture set up the Brambell Committee to enquire into and make recommendations regarding the welfare of such animals. Some, though not all, of their recommendations were embodied in the Agriculture (Miscellaneous Provisions) Act 1968, the main provisions of which were (*a*) to define animal suffering as "unnecessary pain or distress"; (*b*) to give the Minister power to make regulations covering every aspect of animal welfare; (*c*) to provide for Codes of Practice to be prepared for the guidance of stockmen; (*d*) to set up a Farm Animal Welfare Advisory Committee, and (*e*) to provide for the inspection of farms by Ministry veterinary surgeons.

Welcome as these provisions were, some would like to have seen the Act go further in protecting veal calves, poultry and slatted cattle and pigs. The Minister's reply to these criticisms was that there was not in existence sufficient scientific evidence to prove that existing practices led to suffering or stress.

The Church and Nation Report, 1972, discussing these matters in a section on Factory Farming, gave its opinion that wherever conclusive scientific evidence for or against a particular practice was lacking "the balance of judgement should lean towards compassion".

Since that time changes have taken place in the public awareness regarding alternatives to animal meat. Textured vegetable protein has become a common and partially acceptable substitute for meat. Also, in a world hungry for grain, the meat animal has come to be seen as a costly consumer in its function as a protein converter, although in this connection it has to be borne in mind that there are parts of the world where the only economic way of converting vegetation into food is by means of the grazing animal. These trends are unlikely to turn whole populations away from meat eating but they do something to counter the argument that ever increasing quantities of animal meat must be produced at maximum economic efficiency to cater for the insatiable demands of a world on a rising standard of living.

Animals Used in Experimentation

This very emotive subject requires careful handling if the competing claims of scientific research and animal welfare are to be kept in balance.

The Act governing experiments on living animals is still the Cruelty to Animals Act 1876, by which the Home Secretary is given authority to operate a system of licensing of experimenters. At the time of the Act's inception the number of experiments per annum was counted in hundreds, presently it runs at over five million.

Animals as Pets

The British have a name as pet-lovers but the owner-animal relationship takes some curious forms. Some owners over-indulge their pets, killing them with kindness, the range and cost of pet foods and accessories being considerable. Others ill-treat their pets, venting their frustrations and anger on creatures which cannot retaliate. Others again simply neglect them, as with owners who leave their dogs to roam loose while they are at work. Yet others rejoice in owning extra large or exotic pets valuing them perhaps less for themselves than as status symbols. But the majority of owners may be regarded as having a responsible attitude to the keeping of their pets and in return for sensible care, enjoy a rewarding relationship.

The keeping of dogs raises a number of social issues. The emergence of an anti-dog section of public opinion can be attributed to the various nuisances caused by ill-supervised dogs, e.g. the fouling of pavements and parks, and hazard on the roads. Number of dogs that were cherished as pups become the victims of neglect as they grow up and their novelty wears off, while holdiay time each year brings its crop of dogs turned loose to fend for themselves while the family is away.

It would seem that the acquiring of a dog is too easy a process compared with the responsibility of caring for it afterwards. If the annual licence fee were to be substantially increased from its present lowly charge, i.e. to £5 and a proper system of dog registration with name and number tags introduced, as happens in certain other countries, the number of unwanted and ownerless dogs would surely diminish. Moreover, if a licence were required from the moment the dog was acquired rather than at the age of six months, fewer dogs might be bought unthinkingly in the first place.

Universal Declaration of the Rights of Animals
Preamble

Whereas all animals have rights,

Whereas disregard and contempt for the rights of animals have resulted and continue to result in crimes by man against nature and against animals,

Whereas recognition by the human species of the right to existence of other animal species is the foundation of the co-existence of species throughout the animal world,

Whereas genocide has been perpetrated by man on animals and the threat of genocide continues,

Whereas respect for animals is linked to the respect of man for men,

Whereas from childhood man should be taught to observe, understand, respect and love animals,

IT IS HEREBY PROCLAIMED

Article 1

All animals are born with an equal claim on life and the same rights to existence.

Article 2

1. All animals are entitled to respect.
2. Man as an animal species shall not arrogate to himself the right to exterminate or inhumanely exploit other animals. It is his duty to use his knowledge for the welfare of animals.
3. All animals have the right to attention, care and protection of man.

Article 3

1. No animal shall be illtreated or be subject to cruel acts.
2. If an animal has to be killed, this must be instantaneous and without distress.

Article 4

1. All wild animals have the right to liberty in their natural environment, whether land, air or water, and should be allowed to procreate.
2. Deprivation of freedom, even for educational purposes, is an infringement of this right.

Article 5

1. Animals of species living traditionally in a human environment have the right to live and grow at the rhythm and under the conditions of life and freedom peculiar to their species.
2. Any interference by man with this rhythm or these conditions for purposes of gain is an infringment of this right.

Article 6

1. All companion animals have the right to complete their natural life span.
2. Abandonment of an animal is a cruel and degrading act.

Article 7

All working animals are entitled to a reasonable limitation of the duration and intensity of their work, to the necessary nourishment and to rest.

Article 8

1. Animal experimentation involving physical or psychological suffering is incompatible with the rights of animals, whether it be for scientific, medical, commercial or any other form of research.
2. Replacement methods must be used and developed.

Article 9

Where animals are used in the food industry they shall be reared, transported, lairaged and killed without the infliction of suffering.

Article 10

1. No animal shall be exploited for the amusement of man.
2. Exhibitions and spectacles involving animals are incompatible with their dignity.

Article 11

Any act involving the wanton killing of an animal is biocide, that is, a crime against life.

Article 12

1. Any act involving the mass killing of wild animals is genocide, that is, a crime against the species.
2. Pollution or destruction of the natural environment leads to genocide.

Article 13

1. Dead animals shall be treated with respect.
2. Scenes of violence involving animals shall be banned from cinema and television, except for humane education.

Article 14

1. Representatives of movements that defend animal rights should have an effective voice at all levels of government.
2. The rights of animals, like human rights, should enjoy the protection of the law.

Approach to the Political Parties

The following is the full text of the letter sent to the Chairmen of five political parties which had sitting members in the last Parliament, but excluding the Northern Ireland parties:

General Election Co-ordinating Committee for Animal Protection

Chairman:
The Right Hon. Lord Houghton of Sowerby CH.

Secretary
CLIVE HOLLANDS
10 Queensferry Street
Edinburgh EH2 4PG

031-225 2116

ANIMAL PROTECTION
AND POLITICAL PARLIAMENTARY ACTION

A large number of animal welfare and protection societies have come together in a single movement for the one purpose of putting animals into politics. This unity among scores of voluntary societies, large and small, is unique. It reflects the awareness of those bodies that growing public concern is behind the idea of combination for concerted action.

1 . Who we are

The Co-ordinating Committee comprises six joint committees of societies formed to advance specific aims in particular areas of concern. One body whose objects do not fall within one of those groups is shown separately.

Membership of the Co-ordinating Committee is as follows (in alphabetical order)—

172

1. Christian Consultative Council for the Welfare of Animals
2. Committee for the Reform of Animal Experimentation (CRAE).
3. Farm Animal Welfare Co-ordinating Executive (FAWCE).
4. Humane Education Council[1]
5. Joint Advisory Committee on Pets in Society (JACOPIS)[1]
6. National Joint Equine Welfare Committee
and
7. The League Against Cruel Sports.

The comprehensive list of the individual societies in each of the joint bodies is set out in full in *Appendix I.*[2]

2 .Our immediate purpose

We invite the main political parties to include animal protection in some form within their official party policy, and preferably to declare their commitment in a pre-election manifesto.

Our over-riding aim is to persuade the political parties to respond to the growing strength of enlightened public opinion about the treatment and care of animals.

Cruelty to animals is not a private matter. Parliament has legislated about animal welfare and protection for over a century. In recent years however with mounting pressure of "government" business upon Parliamentary time there has been a tendency for successive governments to regard further measures on animal welfare to be "suitable for the Private Member's Bill procedure". This amounts to legislation by lottery and frustration of changes in the law by obstruction or lack of time, or both.

It is therefore crucial to our purpose that the parties should not only have a policy but an intention to promote, facilitate, or support action *by government*.

We therefore seek your acceptance of our contention that animal welfare is the responsibility of government and should not be consigned to the hazard of the Private Member's Bill procedure.

It follows that political parties should regard animal protection as part of their official policy and say what that policy is.

3. *A policy for the political parties.*

The Societies comprising the Co-ordinating Committee have a wide range of aims and objects. Some, the RSPCA in particular, have a broad and comprehensive mission for the prevention of cruelty to animals; others are devoted to the special interests of particular species, like horses and dogs, and some are working for the eradication of cruelty caused by human ignorance, indifference, greed, or simply by what are known as "field sports".

We have endeavoured to set out in one document of reasonable length the matters upon which our member societies invite the political parties to make statements of policy.

This we have done in *Appendix II.*

We do not ourselves put them in order of priority. There are *six* altogether and they appear in *Appendix II* in the order chosen at random. They are:—

A.   Horses: carcase trade for EEC countries; conditions at auctions and sales (Diseases of Animals Act 1950)

B.   Intensive animal husbandry:
       "factory farming" Brambell Report, 1965.

C.   Dogs in the Community:
       Report of Government Working Party 1976.

D.   Experiments on living animals:
       Cruelty to Animals Act 1876.

E.   Blood Sports: live hare coursing and hunting with hounds.

F.   Export of live farm animals:
       O'Brien Report 1974, and recent Report of the Agriculture Departments.

(*Note:* announcement by Ministers are likely on A, C and F before the end of the present Session.)

We must leave any choice of "priorities" to the judgement of the parties themselves. While we aim at "putting animals into politics" it is not for us to enter into discussion of the obvious political and electoral aspects of policy formulation.

Our list of areas of concern explains them all as briefly as we can and asks the questions which each of them suggest being appropriate.

(One omission from the list, which we much regret, relates to the protection of wildlife, especially threatened species, animals and birds in captivity, circuses and the like. The explanation is simply that we have not yet got a "wildlife group" in fully working order, though steps already taken show good promise.)

We invite as many answers as your Party feels able to give. These we suggest should in any event be available for publication, whether or not they are to be included in an election manifesto.

4. *Proposed Royal Commission Animal Protection*
This proposal can be regarded as separate from consideration of the particular matters in *Appendix II*.

It is simply that a Standing Royal Commission on the lines of the existing Royal Commission on the Environment could well be of great help to Parliament in sorting out the complexities of animal welfare and in indicating where action is needed.

The law of animal protection and welfare is at present scattered throughout the Statute Book. A lot of it is to be found in various Agriculture Acts, some in special Acts, and some in attempts at dealing comprehensively with cruelty in general.

One task of a Royal Commission would be to codify the law. Other work very suitable to a Standing Commission would be to study developments relating to the use or treatment of animals which are frequently neglected or even go undiscovered until a major problem emerges. Examples of this kind of thing are to be found in past experience relating to (i) the enormous expansion of the use of animals for substance-testing of commercial products under cover of the Cruelty to Animals Act, 1876, (ii) the rapid growth of intensive animal and poultry husbandry, (iii) growth in the export of live farm animals and in the slaughter of horses for export as carcase meat, (iv) increase in wildlife "safaris" and zoos and (v) the growth of mink and fox-farms. Special *ad hoc* committees of inquiry into some of these proved necessary long after notice should have been taken of the trends in animal use and treatment. By the time these Committees have

175

been appointed, vested interests have combined to resist regulation or control.

In rapidly changing conditions and the extension of protective legislation to human beings in numerous directions (e.g. drug safety, and health and safety in industry, not to mention EEC legislation) the attention and vigilance of a *Standing Commission* on Animal Protection ever ready to inquire and to recommend would be of great value. While in no way do we wish this Commission to be a substitute for needful attention or action by government and still less an excuse for delay, nevertheless it would save a lot of the time of M.P.'s and of animal welfare societies in pursuit of reform. Public opinion lays great store on the independent inquiry and so do governments.

We ask for your support for our proposal to set up a Standing Royal Commission for Animal Protection.

5. *We would like to see you*

We impress upon you that animal welfare is of growing public concern. Some societies have recently found the strongest upsurge of public interest and support in their long experience. There can be no doubt of the importance of this subject to the Political Parties. Electors have their own values, and their outlook on life and the living world. Not all people are preoccupied with material gain; some no doubt vote for their faith in the rights of animals as well as for the rights of man. More and more people will want to know what the political parties stand for in areas of policy too much neglected in the past.

We hope you will welcome this united, comprehensive and fully representative approach at this time, and that you will make full use of the opportunity we offer to consider and discuss what the response of your Party is going to be.

Yours sincerely,

HOUGHTON OF SOWERBY
Chairman

CLIVE HOLLANDS
Secretary

AREAS OF CONCERN

(Note: The following matters are *not* placed in any order *of priority*: *they appear as drawn at random*).

(A)   Horses, Ponies, Mules (Advisory body: The National Joint
Equine Welfare Committee)

The British people are noted for their love of horses. It has been said that the Empire was built upon the back of a horse. Fondness for equine beauty and competitive skill comes out in the popularity of horse-riding, horse-racing, horse trials, show-jumping and so on. Yet there is a squalid side to this romantic picture.

A debate in the House of Lords on 14th December, 1977 brought some of it to light.

New measures and the tightening up of old ones are needed to check growing evils of the trade and traffic in horses. These include:—

(i)   *Horse-dealers, sales and auctions*
Horse-dealers to be licensed by local authorities.
Persons conducting public sales or auctions to be licensed by local authorities.
Public sales of horses to be held only in sale-yards licensed by local authorities.
Conditions at sales and auction yards to be brought within the statutory controls laid down for sales and auctions of farm animals under the Diseases of Animals Act 1950.
The separation of unweaned foals from their dams in auctions sales to be made unlawful.

(ii)   *Slaughter and horse-meat carcase trade*
The export of live horses for slaughter is prohibitied (though see below). Horse-meat for export to EEC countries is permitted from only *four* slaughterhouses which are licensed for this trade. These are situated in

177

Huddersfield, Norwich, Bristol and Crawley.[3] There is no place in Scotland or in Wales. Horses destined for carcase meat for EEC countries are therefore transported for long distances to one (and not necessarily the nearest) of the *four* places above. The numbers are growing and more and more horses are being transported long distances to these four destinations.

This situation requires urgent attention. Horses not for export as carcase meat may be slaughtered anywhere by a licensed horse slaughterer. No central record is kept of the numbers of horses slaughtered outside the four places licensed for the EEC trade.
It is desirable for this information to be collected centrally for horses slaughtered as it already is for farm animals.

(iii) *Export of live horses*
Although the export of live horses for slaughter is unlawful, the safeguards are inadequate.
As a measure of protection against evasion of the law, the Diseases of Animals Acts 1950-1973 ban the export of horses altogether, except for strictly defined purposes, if they are below what is defined in the Act as the "Minimum Protective Value" related to horses of various measurements of height.
These "Minimum Protective Values" have not been raised since 1973: they are quite unrealistic today and should be revised.[4]

The present complexities of Orders, Exceptions, Revocations made under the 1950 Act appear to leave serious loopholes for the export of some horses (e.g. race-horses, and saddle-horses) without conditions or veterinary examinations.

A strong case exists for inquiring into the growing export trade in horses over 14½ hands which are outside the protective conditions of the 1950 Act and subsequent Orders.

178

(iv) *Cruelty by exposure and neglect*

The rising cost of fodder and stabling and shelter is causing an increase in cruelty by exposure and neglect during the months of bad weather.

Many horses and ponies are tethered or hobbled to prevent them straying in search of pastures: others are left without shelter in fields or copses in all weathers.

Casualties due to bad tethering and neglect are on the increase especially during periods of severe weather during last winter. Animals have been rescued by voluntary bodies from starvation and the debilitating effects of prolonged exposure.

Another cause of concern is conditions in some livery yards, improvised staffing, and the letting of impoverished land for grazing.

Cruelty by neglect is as much an offence under existing Acts of Parliament as violence and physical ill-treatment. It may however be less noticeable to the public and the police.

Vigilance is necessary especially in areas where horses and ponies are congregated in unsuitable conditions for sale and slaughter.

Trends are now discernable which are disturbing. One respect in which abuses could be checked would be to follow the example of Portsmouth City Council whose proposed new bye-laws include a ban on tethering of horses, ponies and donkeys in public parks or open spaces.

> Are you in favour of the above proposals and would your Party introduce or support the necessary Parliamentary action?

(B) Intensive animal husbandry (Advisory body: Farm Animal Welfare Co-ordinating Executive)

Some methods of intensive farming cause an unacceptable degree of distress in farm animals. In the light of present knowledge we are opposed to the following farming practices:—

1. The Battery Hen System for egg production.
2. The Deep Litter System where the space provided per hen is less than the following:

   1 sq. metre for laying hens. ½ sq. metre for broiler hens.
3. Veal Calf Production where all or any of the following practices are found:

   (a) individual cubicles are used which severely restrict movement:
   (b) access to roughage is denied:
   (c) lighting is inadequate:
   (d) calves are maintained on totally slatted floors:
   (e) calves are tethered:
   (f) density in multiple calf pens is such that uninhibited movement is prevented.

4. The close tethering of pigs except for a temporary purpose only (such as veterinary examination).
5. The use of cubicles for dry or pregnant sows in which they are kept permanently and are unable to turn round.
6. Systems of pig husbandry where no form of bedding is provided and lighting is inadequate.
7. The castration of piglets destined for fattening for pork.

In some respects existing standards recommended by the several Advisory Bodies concerned are below those in the Brambell Report more than ten years ago.

> Is your Party prepared to have the whole subject of intensive animal husbandry thoroughly reviewed again?

C. Dogs in the Community

An inter-Departmental Committee reported on this in August

1976 (Department of Environment: Report of Working Party on Dogs. H.M.S.O. price 65p)

The Working Party made a number of recommendations, most of which the Joint Advisory Committee on Pets in Society found acceptable.

Our main proposals are:—

1. To transfer responsibility for dealing with stray dogs from the police to local authorities.

2. Local authorities with over 50,000 population should be required to introduce a Dog Warden Scheme to be operated at District Council level.

3. The Dog Warden to be empowered:
    (i)   to obtain information from any person whom he has reasonable cause to believe is the owner of a dog which is of legitimate concern to him (for example, a dog which is causing a disturbance in his area);
    (ii) to ask for the name and address of any person in charge of a dog which is causing or has caused an offence to be committed: and
    (iii) to require a dog owner to produce a valid licence on demand.

4. Local authorities to have power to impound stray dogs (giving full publicity) and to destroy those which are unclaimed, or for which suitable homes cannot be found after a reasonable minimum period.

5. The annual licence fee should be increased to meet a proportion of the cost of the introduction of the Dog Warden Scheme. (We would not contemplate raising the licence fee to more than £5.) All dogs to wear on their collar some form of identification of payment for a current licence.

6. Only guide dogs for the blind should be exempted from the licence fee.

7. Local authorities to be given power to inspect unlicensed premises where it is suspected that dog breeding on a commercial scale is being undertaken.

8. The Breeding of Dogs Act 1973 should be amended to cover puppy farms.

> Do you favour dealing with the problem
> on these lines, and would your Party
> introduce or support the necessary
> legislation?

NOTE:

The Minister of State, Environment has promised an early statement of the Government's intentions about this Report (23/3/78).

(D) Experiments on living animals (Advisory body: Committee for Reform of Animal Experimentation)

These are subject to the provisions of the Cruelty to Animals Act 1876. Our immediate aims are as follows:—

(a) There should be strong, constant emphasis upon the need to restrict procedures likely to cause suffering of any sort, including stress.

(b) A determined effort should be made to restrict the use of animals in procedures which are not strictly for human medical therapeutic purposes such as the testing of cosmetics and toiletries, the testing of weapons and behavioural research.

(c) Progressive restrictions on the use of animals (especially the highly developed species) in favour of non-sentient alternatives should be pursued wherever possible.

(d) Greater importance should be attached to the need for training in, and the application of, the techniques of anaesthesia, analgesia and euthanasia of animals.

(e) Procedures no longer regarded as strictly experimental should not escape the disciplines of the 1876 Act. These include passaging, the transplantation of ova and similar agricultural procedures, the breeding of abnormal animals or animals susceptible to spontaneous diseases, the use of animals in the production of biological substances such as sera and vaccine, and for teaching, training and testing. Other scientific procedures which should not be left to the

182

general laws dealing with cruelty to animals should include any which interfere with the animal's ordinary state of health or well-being (excluding procedures which are part of normal veterinary diagnosis or treatment).

Certain invertebrate species should be brought within amending legislation as also should stock animals being bred and kept for purposes defined in the Act. The 1876 Act should also apply to the Crown.

Noticeable progress has been made in some matters of administration (e.g. the widening of the scope of information required by the Home Secretary for publication in the Annual Return) and also in the fuller use of the Advisory Committee to examine particular experiments (e.g. the L.D. 50—toxicity—testing procedures upon animals has been remitted to them for investigation).

The conditions of granting licenses and certificates to experimenters and the monitoring of their use, is also under review. (The recent conviction of a person at Cupar Sheriff Court for gross abuse of animals and birds for experimental purposes revealed serious cause for concern).

In the present state of the legislative programme the government is not able to promise fresh legislation on this subject, and present discussions are therefore being conducted within the provisions of the 1876 Act.

Legislation is however needed to meet some of our aims, particularly as regards the composition, terms of reference, and powers of the Advisory Committee.

> Is your Party able to endorse the aims set out above and to promise to introduce or support legislation to achieve them?

(E)   "Blood Sports" (Advisory body: League Against Cruel Sports)
Public Opinion polls indicate that a majority of people favour the banning of so-called "blood sports". This description

covers hunting with hounds, otters, stags, hares and foxes. Also included is live-hare coursing.

Most of the surviving otter hunts have gone into voluntary suspension following the Order under the Conservation of Wild Creatures and Wild Plants Act 1975, made effective from 1st January 1978 prohibiting the taking or killing of otters. (The Order was a measure of conservation and not one to stop otter-hunting as such: hunting without taking or killing is still lawful).[5]

On live hare-coursing the present Government introduced a Bill to ban this sport in 1976. It passed the Commons but made no progress in the Lords after the Bill was referred to a Select Committee. The present Government is however still committed to make live hare coursing illegal and promises to re-introduce the Bill "At a suitable opportunity".

What is the view of your Party towards making unlawful

(i)   "blood sports" generally

(ii)   live hare-coursing

(iii) hunting with hounds of:—

        stags and deer

        hares

        otters

        foxes

(F)   Export of live farm animals: (Advisory body: Farm Animal Welfare Co-ordinating Executive)

Animal welfare societies have united to campaign for a total ban on these exports, whether for immediate slaughter or further fattening. Exports have been rising sharply and the export of calves has increased by more than half during 1977. Last year Ministers appointed a working group of officials in the agricultural departments to review the live export trade, following instances of considerable hardship and cruelty obtained from trails by the Special Investigation Unit of the RSPCA and other bodies.

184

That report—to which outside bodies gave evidence—was published on 23rd March, 1978. It is now open for comment before the government comes to a view. FAWCE believes the report to be biased and unbalanced and written from the standpoint of finding evidence to support a continuation of this trade.

In a statement of its position on live exports, FAWCE said: "We believe there is no way in which the British Government or any other government can guarantee that the various national, EEC and Council of Europe laws, rules, regulations and directives can be fully and consistently enforced to ensure that animals are in all cases treated in accordance with their various provisions."

FAWCE believes that the live export trade is bad for the agricultural industry as a whole, threatens jobs in abbatoirs and the leather, tanning and associated industries, as well as leading to rising imports of hides, skins and offals.

The economic case for the trade is not made out because the total value of all farm animals exported for slaughter or further fattening in 1977 was about £65 million—enough to pay for just 22 day's worth of imports of meat and meat preparations.

In common with the British Veterinary Association, and indeed the O'Brien Committee report, FAWCE believes that animals should be slaughtered as near to the point of production as possible.

> What is the view of your Party to this?

Notes

Introduction

1. Cohen, *Pet Animals and Society* (Baillière Tindall, 1975).
2. *Veterinary Record* 2:3:68.

Chapter I

1. Harrison, *Animal Machines* (Vincent Stuart, 1964).
2. *Report of the Technical Committee to Enquire into the Welfare of Animals kept under Intensive Livestock Husbandry Systems (Comnd. 2836)* (HMSO, 1965).
3. Personal communication to the author 26:9:78.
4. Fox, *Between Animal and Man* (Blond Briggs, 1976).
5. *Sunday Times* 21:5:78.
6. *Sunday Times* 5:12:76.
7. On experimentation involving human subjects, see Papworth, *Human Guineapigs* (Routledge and Kegan Paul, 1967).
8. Metcalfe, *The British Cruelty to Animals Act, 1876—Its Origin, History, and Scope.*
9. *Houghton/Platt Memorandum to the Home Secretary* (May, 1976).
10. *General Practitioner* 20:4:79.
11. *Scotsman* 6:9:78 and *Evening Herald* (Glasgow) 6:9:78.
12. *Journal of Animal Production* 27 *(1978),* p.43.
13. *Statistics of Experiments on Living Animals (Cmnd. 7628)* (HMSO, 1978).
14. *The Sensitive Scientist* (SCM Press, 1978).
15. Jordan and Ormrod, *The Last Great Wild Beast Show* (Constable, 1978).
16. Carding, *Pet Animals and Society* (Baillière Tindall, 1975).

Chapter II

1. Brown, *Who cares for Animals?* (Heinemann, 1974).
2. Moss, *The Valiant Crusade* (Cassell, 1961).
3. Rybot, *It began before Noah* (Michael Joseph, 1972).
4. Douglas Hume, *The Mind-Changers* (The Hume Books Trust, 1939).
5. The Life of Frances Power Cobbe published by Richard Bentley and Son, 1894.
6. Vyvyan, *In Pity and in Anger* (Michael Joseph, 1969).

Detailed information on the founding of the first animal societies is also to be found in the following books:

187

Westacott, *A century of Vivisection and Anti-Vivisection* (Daniel, 1949); Niven, *The History of the Humane Movement* (Johnson, 1967); *Vyvyan, The Dark Face of Science* (Michael Joseph, 1971); Ryder, *Victims of Science* (Davis-Poynter, 1975); Hosali, *The Spana Story* (SPANA 1978); and Judith Hampson's Ph.D. thesis (University of Leicester 1978), *Animal Experimentation, 1876-1976.*

Chapter III

1. This Act was repealed by the Mortmain and Charitable Uses Act of 1888, but the Preamble to the earlier Act was retained.

2. *Hansard,* House of Lords 21:3:60.

3. *Report of the Committee on the Law and Practice relating to Charitable Trusts.*

4. *Charity and Fund-Raising Review* August, 1970.

5. *Idem* June-July, 1972.

6. *Tax Cases, 28,* Pt. 7.

7. *Tenth Report of the House of Commons Select Committee on Expenditure* (1975).

8. *Charity Law and Voluntary Organisations, the Report of the Goodman Committee* (Bedford Square Press, 1976).

Chapter IV

1. In law, the term "animals" includes all creatures not belonging to the human race. They are then broadly divided into two groups, domestic and wild. Domestic animals include all those domestic or tame animals as by habit or training live in association with man. Wild animals include not only those which are savage by nature but also those of a more mild or timid nature which cannot be classed as domestic or tame. But a domestic animal which reverts to a wild state is no longer domestic but wild. (On this, see Sandys-Winsch, *Animal Law* (Shaw and Sons, 1978).

2. *Scotsman* 14:8:79.

3. *Exodus 21, 8.*

4. 9 Geo. 1 c.22.

5. *Animals' Defender and Zoophilist* June, 1921.

6. Westacott, *Supra*, notes to chapter II.

7. The *Animals (Transit and General) Orders, 1895 and 1904,* and the *Exportation of Horses Order, 1898* relating to the carriage of animals by land and sea; the *Diseases of Animals Act, 1894* and the *Injured Animals Act, 1894* replaced the Act of 1907.

8. This Act was subsequently repealed and replaced by the *Protection of Animals (Anaesthetics) Act, 1954.*

9. University of Sheffield, unpublished thesis.

10. *Animals*, (Massacheusetts SPCA) November-December, 1977.

Chapter V

1. An independent panel of inquiry under the chairmanship of Charles Sparrow, Q.C., was set up following a resolution at the Society's A.G.M. in June 1973. The brief of the panel was to inquire into any complaints about the Society's management, the conduct of its affairs generally, and its Constitution and rules. The report of the panel was published in November 1974 and made sweeping recommendations for changes in the management and administration of the RSPCA. It was hardly complimentary about the affairs of the Society.

2. UFAW's decision was not based on opposition to the proposal as such but rested on the grounds that the Year intended to seek commercial sponsorship.

Chapter VI

1. *Spectator* 17:9:77.

2. *Animal Welfare* July-August, 1977.

3. *The LD 50 Test—Evidence for submission to the Home Office Advisory Committee, prepared by CRAE, the Committee for the Reform of Animal Experimentation,* (August, 1977).

Chapter VIII

1. Copies of this sermon are still available from the author at 10, Queensferry Street, Edinburgh.

2. *Listener* 19:5:77.

3. Paterson and Ryder (eds), *Animal Rights—a Symposium* (Centaur Press, 1979) (This book is obtainable from the RSPCA at the price of £6.50).

Chapter IX

1. *Daily Mail* 12:7:76.

2. *New Scientist* 19:8:76. This first appeared in *New Scientist*, London, the weekly review of science and technology.

3. *Lancet* 25th September, 1976.

4. Church of Scotland, *Report to the General Assembly,* 1977.

Chapter X

1. The following were signatories to the Houghton/Platt Memorandum:
House of Lords: Lord Houghton; Lord Platt
House of Commons: Mr F. A. Burden; Miss J. Fookes; Mr K. Lomas.
Others: Dr K. Pedler; Mr R. D. Ryder; Mr W. J. Jordan; Mr C. Hollands.

2. "This crude and cruel procedure consists of determining the dosage level at which 50 per cent of the test animals survive and 50 per cent die. Almost by definition one is establishing a level of dosage at which the animals will be made ill, most of them lingering near death before succumbing or surviving". (Godlovitch and Harris, *Animals, Men, and Morals* (Gollancz, 1971).

3. *Report on the LD 50 test* (Home Office, 1979).

4. *Hansard,* House of Commons 6:7:78.

5. *Sunday Telegraph* 24:9:78.

6. *Western Mail* 11:8:77.

7. Commission of the European Communities, *Review of pre-slaughter stunning in the EC, Information on Agriculture* March, 1977. *Report of the Working Party on Slaughterhouse Hygiene,* (Environmental Health Officers Association, 1977). National Food Administration, *Hearing on Pre-slaughter Stunning,* (Uppšala, 1978).

Chapter XI

1. Ligue Internationale des Droits de l' Animals, *Report* (1978).

2. Paterson and Ryder (eds) *Animal Rights,* op. cit.

3. The subscribing societies were: the Animal Welfare Trust; the British Union for the Abolition of Vivisection; the League against Cruel Sports; the St Andrew Animal Fund; and the Scottish Society for the Prevention of Vivisection.

4. *Spectator* 17:9:77.

5. *Sunday Telegraph* 18:7:76.

Chapter XII

1 As there was no joint consultative body representing wild animals, the LACS was invited to participate in the campaign to advise on blood sports.

2. NOP Market Research Ltd, *Public Attitudes towards Hunting with Hounds* (June 1978).

3. *Field* 15:11:78.

4. *Shooting Times and Country Magazine* 11—17:1:79.

Chapter XIII

1. *Daily Telegraph* 4:10:78.

2. *Contemporary Review* March, 1979.

3. This document is available from the Labour Party, Transport House, Smith Square, London, or from 10, Queensferry Street, Edinburgh.

Chapter XIV

1. *Scotsman* 28:3:79.

2. Excerpts from the debate are taken from *Hansard*, House of Commons, Vol 964, 23:3:79.

3. The proposed Council was to have the power to review existing legislation and recommend legislative or other action on any animal welfare matter. It was also to have the power to propose improvements in the existing advisory machinery. *Hansard*, House of Commons, 22:3:79.

190

Chapter XV

1. *Economist* 31:3:79.
2. *Poultry World* 15:2:79.
3. *Ibid* 16:11:78.
4. *Farmers Guardian* 27:10:78.
5. *Farmers Weekly* 22:9:78.
6. *Insight*, (NFU) 17:3:79.
7. *Veterinary Record* 7:4:79.
8. *Field* 29:11:78.
9. *Nursing Times* 8:3:79.
10. *Ibid* 29:3:79.

Chapter XVI

1. *Scotsman* 14:9:78.
2. *Guardian* 22:1:79.

Chapter XVII

1. MAFF, Press Notice 25:7:79.
2. *Hansard*, House of Commons 8:11:79.
3. *New Scientist* 25:10:79.
4. *Proposals For Change In the Legislation Governing the Use of Live Animals in Research, Experiments and Other Laboratory Purposes.* CRAE'S memorandum to the Home Secretary, November 1979.
5. *British Farmer*, (NFU) 7:7:79.

Chapter XVIII

1. *Cambridge News* 10:7:79.
2. *Evening Express* 12:9:79 (Aberdeen).
3. *Sunday Telegraph* 2:12:79.
4. *Scotsman* 31:8:79.
5. *Veterinary Record* 22:12:79.
6. Chairman's address to the A.G.M. of the RSPCA 22nd June, 1979.
7. *Field* 29:11:78.
8. Ryder and Paterson (eds) *Animal Rights*, op. cit.

Chapter XIX

1. Cloete, *The Curve and the Tusk*. (Collins, 1953).
2. *Contemporary Review* March, 1979.
3. *Hansard*, House of Commons 23:3:79.

4. *Time Out* 20:9:79.

5. Duffy, *I want to go to Moscow*, (Hodder and Stoughton, 1973). Reprinted by permission of Hodder and Stoughton Limited. (Copyright, Maureen Duffy).

6. Davis, *Leviathan* (Michael Joseph, 1976).

7. Hamilton, *The Beagle Brigade* (Exposition Press, 1980).

APPENDICES

1. The letter to the political parties was sent to the Chairmen of the parties before the withdrawal of the Joint Advisory Committee on Pets in Society and the Humane Education Council.

2. Appendix I has been omitted in the text as it merely lists the member societies of the joint consultative bodies.

3. These are now five slaughterhouses licensed to slaughter for the E.E.C. The additional one being located at Nantwich.

4. With effect from 27th December 1978, the Minimum Protective Values have been substantially increased which should discourage export of live horses for meat.

5. This order only applies to England and Wales—hunting and killing otters in Scotland is still permitted.

INDEX

Acts of Parliament
  Agriculture Acts 31
  Agriculture (Miscellaneous Provisions) Acts 31
  Agriculture (Miscellaneous Provisions) Act, 1968 31
  Agriculture (Spring Traps) Scotland Act, 1969 25
  Animal Boarding Establishments Act, 1963 31
  Animals (Anaesthetics) Act, 1919 31
  Animals (Cruel Poisons) Act, 1962 79
  Badgers Act, 1973 32
  "Black Act of 1722" 26
  Breeding of Dogs Act, 1973 31, 181
  Conservation of Seals Act, 1970 32
  Conservation of Wild Creatures and Wild Plants Act, 1975 32, 78, 184
  Cruelty to Animals Act, 1876 8, 27, 39, 40, 42, 62, 73, 119, 134, 157, 158, 174, 182, 183
  Deer (Scotland) Act, 1959 32
  Diseases of Animals Act, 1894 Notes, Ch. IV, Note 7
  Diseases of Animals Act, 1950 31, 174, 178
  Diseases of Animals Acts, 1950-1973 178
  Dogs Act, 1906 31
  Games Acts 32
  Injured Animals Act, 1894 Notes, Ch. IV, Note 7
  Pests Act, 1954 32
  Pet Animals Act, 1951 31
  Preamble to an Act, 1601 21
  Protection of Animals Act, 1911 30, 158
  Protection of Animals (Anaesthetics) Act, 1954 Notes, Ch.IV, Note 8
  Protection of Animals (Scotland) Act, 1912 9, 31, 158
  Protection of Birds Act, 1954 32
  Representation of the People Act, 1949 121
  Riding Establishments Acts, 1964 and 1970 31
  Sea Birds Protection Act, 1869 26
  Slaughterhouses Act, 1974 31
  Veterinary Surgeons Act, 1966 32
  Wild Animals in Captivity Act, 1900 30
Advisory Committee on Animal Experiments 132, 134
Agricultural Research Council, Scotland 10, 144
Albrighton Animal Rescue Team 162
Alexander-Sinclair, J.A.C. 41, 42, 84
American International Fund for Animal Welfare see International Fund for Animal Welfare
Anaesthesia, Analgesia, Euthanasia 182
Anglican Society for the Welfare of Animals 19, 66, 149, 162
Angling 122
Anglo-Italian Society for the Protection of Animals 19, 162
Anglo-Spanish Animal Welfare Society 19, 162
Anglo-Venetian Society 19
Animal activists 152, 153, 154
Animal Advocates Information Service 86, 92, 115
Animal Aid 153
Animal Defence Society 18
Animal Liberation Front 153
Animal Life Brigade 162
"Animal lovers" xix
Animal Protection Action Fund (proposed) 156
"Animal Rights" Symposium, Trinity College, Cambridge 72, 85, 150, Notes, Ch. VIII, Note 3
Animal welfare xviii, xix, 41, 105-114, 138

193

Animal Welfare Group, Parliament-
see Parliamentary Animal Welfare
Group
Animal welfare movement 13-20, 151-
156
Animal Welfare Trust 57, 162,
Notes Ch. XI, Note 3
Animal Welfare Year xvii,xviii, 23,
37-87, 92, 107, 119, 134, 137, 147,
148, 149, 157-164
events 67-72
fund-raising 58, 159
organising committee 41, 42, 43, 44,
45
publicity 61-66, 85, 86
Animals,
dead 171
exotic 39, 167
farm (food) 40, 41, 110, 122, 124,
131, 132, 158, 164, 166, 170
laboratory 39, 41, 42, 132, 135,
158, 170
performing 11, 40, 79, 110, 170,
174
pet xix, 11, 12, 39, 41, 42, 114,
124, 158, 164, 167, 168, 170
pet—abandoned and unwanted 39,
42, 164, 167, 168, 180
pet—responsibility of owners 42,
167
pet—population control xix, 124
sporting 39
strays xix, 39, 42, 167, 168, 181
trained (to do menial work) 12
wild 11, 40, 41, 42, 80, 81, 125, 170,
174, 175
wild—trapped for laboratories 42
wild—placing on public show 42
wild—killing for commercial use
42
wild—methods of control 125
working 170
cruelty to 169, 173, 179
respect for 169
rights of 109, 110, 151, 152, 169-171
Animals Defence League 19
Animals' Vigilantes 47
Anti-Steel-Toothed Trap Committee
18
Appleton, Dr. 16
Aspinall, John 69
Association of British Anti-Vivisection
Societies xviii

Atkins, Ronald, M.P. 112

Badgers, gassing of 113
Band of Mercy 153
Barnes Wildlife and Animal Welfare
Group 57, 162
Bartlett, Canon 68
Battersea Dogs Home—see Dogs
Home, Battersea
Battery hens 4, 116, 145, 146, 166, 180
Bear baiting 14, 26
Beauty Without Cruelty (International)
20, 41, 56, 162
Beauty Without Cruelty (Scotland) 46,
69, 162
Belfast Society for the Prevention of
Cruelty to Animals—see Ulster
Society for the Prevention of Cruelty
to Animals
Bell, Ernest 19
Bennett, Andrew, M.P. 112
Bentham, Jeremy 3
Benyon, A. Gwyn 44
Biocide 171
Blake, William 14
Bleakholt Animal Sanctuary 162
Blood sports 7, 29, 42, 92, 93, 94, 111,
113, 119, 122, 123, 124, 125, 174,
183, 184
Blue Cross (see also Dumb Friends'
League) 19, 162
Bovine tuberculosis 113
Boscawen, Robert, M.P. 114
Braine, Sir Bernard M.P. 79
Brambell, Prof. Rogers 4
Brambell Report 4, 110, 174
Bransby Home of Rest for Horses 83,
162
British Association for the Advance-
ment of Science 9, 11
British Council of Anti-Vivisection
Societies xviii
British Field Sports Society 123, 124
British Horse Society 94, 95, 162
British Union for the Abolition of
Vivisection 18, 46, 50, 57, 73, 80,
119, 137, 148, 162, Notes Ch. XI
Note 3
British Veterinary Association 78, 94,
138, 144, 185
British Veterinary Association—
Welfare Advisory Group 138

Brooke Hospital for Animals, Cairo 19, 162
Broome, the Rev. Arthur 15
Brown, Anthony 13 Notes, Ch. II, Note 1
Brown, Bill 136
Browning, Robert 14
Bull Baiting 14, 25
Burden, F.A., M.P. xvii, 37, 39, 41, 57, 83, 109, 157, Notes, Ch. X, Note 1
Burns, Robert 14
Bywater, Harold 56

Cairney, John 69
Calder, Comm. Francis 15
Callaghan, James, M.P. 97, 99
Captive Animals Defence League— see Animals Defence League
Captive Animals Protection Society 19, 162
Carding, A. Notes, Ch. I, Note 16
Carnarvon, Lord 2, 17, 28, 29
Carpenter, Dr. Edward, Dean of Westminster 44, 80
Catholic Study Circle for Animal Welfare 19, 41, 162
Cats xix 9, 145, 164
Cats Protection League 18, 41, 46, 47, 56, 57, 66, 162
Cattle 131
Central Council for Societies for the Prevention of Cruelty to Animals in Scotland 46, 162
Central Dog Registry 162
Chambers, Joan 97
Chanin, Paul 78
Chapman, Pat 85, 115
Charitable Status 21-24
Charity Commissioners 21, 22, 23, 43, 137
Chemical Industries Association 118
Chickens' Lib 100
Church of England 14, 65
Church of Scotland 65, 165-168, Notes, Ch. IX, Note 4
Cicero 13
Christian Consultative Council for the Welfare of Animals 80, 81, 172
Cloete, Stuart 152, Notes, Ch. XIX, Note 1
Cobbe, Frances Power 16, 17, 18, 29

Cock fighting 14, 26
Cohen, D. Notes, Intro., Note 1
Coleridge, the Hon. Stephen 17
Commission of the European Communities Notes, Ch. X, Note 7
Committee for the Reform of Animal Experimentation 50, 73, 74, 75, 76, 81, 132, 134, 135, 137, 142, 143, 146, 147, 148, 151, 172, 182, Notes, Ch. VI, Note 3, Ch. XVII, Note 4
Compassion in World Farming 20, 41, 47, 56, 66, 162
Conference of Animal Welfare Societies 162
Conference of Scottish Animal Welfare Societies, Edinburgh 37, 157
Conservation xviii, 32, 123
Conservative (Party) Ecology Group 126
Co-ordinating Animal Welfare 153
Corbett, Robin, M.P. 77, 99, 110
Cork Society for the Prevention of Cruelty to Animals 16
Cosmetic testing on animals (see Experiments, cosmetic)
Council for Animal Welfare (proposed) 110, 111, 112, 114, 121, 134
Council of Europe Convention for the Protection of Laboratory Animals 135
Council of Justice to Animals 19
Course, Richard 93, 97, 98, 99, 124
Cowper, William 14
Cross, R. A. 29
Crusade Against All Cruelty to Animals 46, 162

Darling, Sir Frank Fraser 6
Dartmoor Livestock Protection Society 20
Davis, John Gordon 154, Notes, Ch. XIX, Note 6
Delane, Mr. 28
Dept. of the Environment's Working Party on Dogs 78, 174, 181
Desai, His Excellency Morarji 84
Destruction of natural environment 171
Dewhurst, Olive 70
Dexter, Jeannette 54
Dickin, Mrs. 18
Dog Aid Society of Scotland 162

195

Dog Wardens 124, 181
Dogs xix, 164, 174, 180, 181
Dogs, Licensing of 181
Dogs Home, Battersea 16, 162
Dolphins 33, 79
Domestic Fowl 131
Donaldson, Lord 49
Donkeys 164, 179
Dowding, Lady 20
Dr. Hadwen Trust 162
Duffy, Maureen 154, Notes, Ch. XIX, Note 5
Dumb Friends' League (see also Blue Cross) 19
Dundee Society for the Prevention of Cruelty to Animals 16

Eagles, Julie 119
Edinburgh Cat Protection League 162
Edinburgh Dog and Cat Home 162
Elephants 152
Emmans, Gerry 116
Endangered Species 42, 79, 86, 122, 123
Erskine of Restormel, Lord 15, 25
Euthanasia 182
Exodus, Book of 25
Experiments 9, 10, 11, 63, 144, 145, 182, 183
   cold resistance in newborn lambs 10, 144
   kittens' eyes 145
   grafting monkeys' heads 9
   maternal affection in rabbits 10
   maternal deprivation in monkeys 10
   play behaviour and prey-catching ability of the domestic feline 9, 183
   sciatic nerves—mice and rats 145
   toxicity in monkeys 145
   will to live in rats 10
   cosmetic (cosmetic testing on animals) 8, 65, 120
Export of live (food) animals 40, 41, 77, 110, 112, 119, 122, 123, 124, 131, 174, 175, 177, 178, 184, 185

Farm Animal Welfare Advisory Committee 110
Farm Animal Welfare Co-ordinating Executive 69, 77, 81, 110, 131, 146, 147, 151, 172, 179, 184, 185

Farm Animal Welfare Council 132, 133, 134
Farming 3, 41, 123
   factory 3, 4, 40, 41, 116, 124, 138, 166, 174, 175, 179, 180
   non-intensive 5
Farnham & Aldershot Animal Rescue Service 162
Fauna Preservation Society 86
Feline Defence League 18
Fellowship of Life 162
Follett, Alison Lady 56
Food Animals Conference 77
Fookes, Janet, M.P. 50, 112, 158, Notes, Ch. X, Note 1
Ford, Margaret E. 17
Ford, Richard 32
Fox, George 14
Fox, Dr. Michael 6, Notes, Ch.I, Note 4
Foxes 7, 184
Francis of Assisi, St. 68
Friends' Anti-Vivisection Association (Friends' Animal Welfare and Anti-Vivisection Society, Quaker Concern for Animals) 19, 66, 162
Friends of Animals League 162
Friends of the Earth 78, 79
Fry, Peter, M.P. 135
Fry Bill—see Protection of Animals (Scientific Purposes) Bill
Fund for the Replacement of Animals in Medical Experiments 20, 41, 56, 163
Funnell, Fay 107
Furs 5, 6, 41

Galitzine, Prince Alexander 91
Galitzine, Anne Princess 56, 57, 64
Gardner, the Hon. Juliet 27
General Election Co-ordinating Committee for Animal Protection 91-95, 97, 98, 99, 100, 107, 108, 109, 115, 120, 121, 124, 125, 126, 127, 137, 148, 152
Genocide 169, 171
Godlovitch and Harris Notes, Ch.X, Note 2
Goodman Committee 24
Gould, Dr. Donald 9
Greek Animal Welfare Society 19
Gunn, Brian 97, 99, 107, 148

Halsbury, Lord 134, 135
Halsbury Bill—see Laboratory Animals Protection Bill (HL)
Hamilton, Comm. Innes 155, Notes, Ch. XIX, Note 7
Hamilton, Comm. Innes and Mrs. 70
Hamilton and Brandon, Nina, Duchess of 18, 45
Hamilton and Brandon, the Dowager Duchess of 44, 45
Hampson, Dr. Judith 136, Notes, Ch. II.
Hanchett-Stamford, Derek 57, 79
Hare Coursing 122, 125, 184
Harman, Col. King 29
Harrison, Ruth 4, 116, Notes, Ch. I, Note 1
Hastings, Stephen, M.P. 111
Hawtrey, Eric 83
Hayman, Damaris 69
Heath, Edward, M.P. 100
Hegarty, Mrs. D. 41, 56
Heim, Dr. Alice 9, 11
Herbert, Auberon, M.P. 27, 28
Herring, Betty 69
Heswall and District Animal Welfare Society 163
Heuse, Georges 84
Hicks, Sidney 57
Hobhouse, J. S. 37
Hodgson, Miss C. 41
Hogan, Drs. George and Frances 16
Hogarth, William 14
Hollands, Clive 41, 115, 160, 176, Notes, Ch.X, Note 1
Hollands, Fay 70
Home for Lost and Starving Dogs, Battersea—see Dogs Home, Battersea
Home of Rest for Horses 19
Home Office Committee on the 1876 Act 110
Home Secretary's Advisory Committee (on LD50) 74
Horses & Ponies Protection Society 163
cruelty by exposure and neglect 179
dealers, sales and auctions 177
export of live 178
slaughter of 11, 76, 77, 177, 178
transport for slaughter 65, 76, 77, 178

ponies, mules 19, 40, 41, 110, 164, 174, 175, 177, 179
Hosali, Kate and Anna 19, Ch.II, Houghton Award 137
Houghton of Sowerby, Lord 44, 45, 49, 62, 70, 73, 76, 85, 91, 92, 100, 101, 107, 117, 118, 119, 120, 127, 137, 143, 152, 164, 176, Ch.X, Note 1
Houghton/Platt Memorandum 8, 62, 63, 73, Ch.I, Note 9, Ch.X, Note 1
House of Commons Select Committee on Expenditure 23, 24
Howletts Zoo Park 69
Hoyle, E. Douglas M.P. 79
HRH Prince Charles 44, 45
HRH Prince Philip 45
HRH Queen Elizabeth II 79
Hulbert-Powell, E.C.L. 49
Humane Education Council 80, 81, 94, 95, 147, 151, 172
Humane Education Society 163
Humane Research Trust 163
Humane Slaughter Association 19
Hume, Maj. C. W. 18
Hume, E. Douglas 16, 19, Ch.II, Note 4
Hunt, Peter 83
Hunt Saboteurs Association 123, 153

International Association Against Painful Experiments on Animals 47
International Fund for Animal Welfare 93
International League for Animal Rights 84
International League for the Protection of Horses 163
International Society for the Protection of Animals 41, 56, 163
International Whaling Commission xviii
Irvine, Charles, M.P. 69

J. Arthur Rank Group Charity 53
Jack London Club (Performing and Captive Animals Defence League) see also Performing Animals Defence League 19
Jacobs, David 68

Japan Animal Welfare Society 19, 163
Joint Advisory Committee on Pets in Society 78, 81, 92, 93, 172, 181
Joint Otter Group Conference 78
Jordan, W. J. Ch. X, Note 1
Jordan, W. J. and Ormrod Stefan 11, Ch.I, Note 15

Kendall, Ena 61
Kennel Club 78
Kent, Duchess of 45
Kimball, Marcus, M.P. 113
King, Angela, Ottaway, John and Potter, Angela 78

Laboratory Animals Protection Bill (HL). 135, 142
Latham, Arthur, M.P. 109
Latto, Dr. Gordon 70
Latto, Joan 70
Law and animal welfare 25-33, 85, 112, 173, 175, 183
Law and animals 171, Ch.IV, Note 1
Lawson Tait Medical and Scientific Research Trust 163
LD 50 Test 74, 75, 183, Ch.VI, Note 3, Ch.X, Note 2
League Against Cruel Sports 41, 42, 46, 92, 93, 94, 97, 125, 126, 127, 137, 163, 173, 183, Ch.XI, Note 3, Ch.XII, Note 1
League for the Prohibition of Cruel Sports 19
Lind-af-Hageby, Miss 18
Lindo, Miss 19
Linzey, the Rev. Andrew 80
Littlewood Enquiry 134
Liverpool Society for Preventing Wanton Cruelty to Brute Animals 15
Liverpool Young Vegetarians 69
Lomas, K., M.P. Ch.X, Note 1
London Anti-Vivisection Society 17
Lord Dowding Fund for Humane Research 47
Lothian Cat Rescue 20
Luetchford, D. 41

McMillan, Bill 118, 119
M'naghten, Lord 22
McNee, Patrick 70
Major, Mrs. 16
Mammal Society 78

Martin, Richard (Humanity Dick) 15, 25, 26
Massereene and Ferrard, the Viscount 44, 70
Mellanby, Prof. Kenneth 79
Metcalfe, Harvey xvii, Ch.I, Note 8
Meth, Prof. 33
Methodists 14
Mills, Peter, M.P. 110
Mink and fox farms 5, 175
Moles, poisoning with strychnine 79
Montefiore, Hugh, Bishop of Birmingham 68
More, Jasper, M.P. 113
Morris, Johnny 70
Moss, A. W. 13, 30, Ch.II, Note 2
Movement Against Cruel Experiments 163
Mylne, Christopher xvii, 37

National Anti-Vivisection Society 17 47, 48, 49, 50, 73, 93, 97, 137, 148
National Anti-Vivisection Society v. the Inland Revenue Commissioners, 1948 22
National Canine Defence League 18, 41, 57, 163
National Consultative Committee for Animal Protection 127, 137, 151
National Council for Animals Welfare 163
National Council of Women— Welfare of Animals Committee— see Welfare of Animals Committee (National Council of Women)
National Dog Rescue Co-ordinating Committee 163
National Equine Defence League 18
National Farmers' Union 115, 116, 117, 138, 145
National Joint Equine Welfare Committee 76, 81, 93, 94, 151, 173, 177
National Otter Survey 78
National Petition for the Protection of Animals 136
National Society for the Abolition of Cruel Sports 19, 163
Nature Conservancy Council 49, 78
"Necessary" and "unnecessary" suffering 30, 31, 32, 75, 166
Newsom, John 16

Newton, Tony, M.P. 114
Niven, Charles D. Notes, Ch.II.
Northern Counties Horse Protection
   Society 163

O'Brien Committee Report, 1974 174,
   185
Order of Nature 84
Orders
   Animals (Transit and General)
   Orders, 1895, 1904 Notes, Ch.IV,
   Note 7
   Exportation of Horses Order, 1898
   Notes, Ch.IV, Note 7
Osborn, Stanley 57
Otter Haven Trust 86
Otters 32, 78, 86, 184
"Oxford Three" 153

Papworth, M.H. Notes, Ch. I, Note 7
Parfitt, Trevor 116, 117
Parker of Waddington, Lady 44
Parliamentary Animal Welfare Group
   38, 62
Parratt, Arthur E. 41, 56
Paterson, David 70, 80, 127
Paterson, D. and Ryder, Richard D.
   Notes, Ch.VIII, Note 3, Ch.XI,
   Note 2
Pedigree Petfoods Education Service
   66
Pedler, Dr. Kit Notes, Ch.X, Note 1
Peoples' Dispensary for Sick Animals
   18, 49, 163
Performing Animals Defence League
   (see also Jack London Club) 19, 46,
   57, 79, 163
Pet Animal Welfare Societies 78
Pet Food Manufacturers Association
   78
Pigeon shooting 29, 30
Pigs 131, 164
Pigs—intensive systems 5, 146, 166,
   180
Pit ponies 19
Platt, Colin 41, 56
Platt, Lord 62, Notes, Ch. X, Note 1
Plutarch 13
Pollution 171
Pollution, oil 112, 113
Ponies of Britain 41, 57, 66, 163
Poole, Gennie 55, 70
Port Lympne Wildlife Sanctuary 69

Porter, Lord 23, 24
Prior, James, M.P. 100
Protect Our Livestock Group 69, 163
Protection of Animals (Scientific
   Purposes) Bill (Fry Bill) 135, 136,
   142
Pulteney, Sir William 14, 25
Putting Animals Into Politics xvii, 85,
   91-127, 136, 137, 142, 147, 149, 155
   approaches to political parties 172-
   185
   co-ordinating committee 172, 173
   "opposition" publicity 115-120
   parliamentary debate 108-114
   party statements 101, 102, 103
   party manifestos 122, 123

Quaker Concern for Animal Welfare—see Friends' Animal Welfare
   and Anti-Vivisection Society
Quakers 14
Queen Victoria 15, 28

Reece, Sir Gerald 38, 44, 45
Rees, Merlyn, M.P. 73
Reid, Beryl 70
Renton, Sir David, M.P. 108, 109
Research Defence Society 22, 63, 118,
   134
Research, humane alternative methods
   39, 41, 42, 65, 170, 182
Research (experiments) non-medical
   39, 42, 63, 65, 120, 170, 175, 182
Roberts, Peter 41, 56
Romans, Book of 165
Rooker, Jeff, M.P. 108, 109, 152
Roosmalecocq, Col. A. H. 41, 57
Ross, Stephen, M.P. 112, 113
Royal College of Veterinary Surgeons
   138
Royal Commission on Animal Welfare
   /Protection (proposed) 83, 84, 108,
   111, 134, 175, 176
Royal Commission on Vivisection 16,
   27, 31
Royal Society for the Prevention of
   Cruelty to Animals 13, 16, 37, 38,
   41, 44, 46, 56, 62, 66, 69, 72, 80,
   100, 106, 107, 112, 124, 125, 127,
   132, 133, 135, 137, 146, 147, 148,
   157, 163, 17? 184, Notes, Ch. V,
   Note 1, Ch. XVIII, Note 6

Royal Society for the Prevention of Cruelty to Animals—"Charter for Animals" 124, 125

Royal Society for the Protection of Birds 18, 49, 80, 94, 95

Rybot, Doris 14, 20, Notes, Ch.II, Note 3

Ryder, Richard D, 69, 70, 85, 91, 147, 148, Notes, Ch. II, Ch. X, Note 1,

Sainsbury, Dr. David 116

Scott, Prof. G. 144

Scott-Henderson Committee 32

Scottish Anti-Vivisection Society 17, 40, 46, 163

Scottish Society for the Prevention of Cruelty to Animals, Edinburgh 16

Scottish Society for the Prevention of Vivisection xvi, xvii, 17, 41, 46, 55, 66, 91, 93, 137, 148, 163, Ch.XI, Note 3

Scottish Society for the Total Suppression of Vivisection 17

Scottish Wildlife Trust 163

Seager, Maj. R. F. 37, 38, 161

Seals, grey 6, 112

Seals, harp 6, 79, 112

Shaftesbury, Lord 27

Shakespeare 8

Shaw, Arnold, M.P. 113

Shooting 122

Sidmouth Animal Welfare Group 163

Silkin, John, M.P. 110

Singer, Peter 72

Sion, Jeffrey 70

Sitwell, Nigel 47

Slaughter 19, 41, 77, 78, 124, 131, 132, 146, 170

Slaughter, pre-stunning 77, 78, 131, 146, Notes, Ch. X, Note 7

Snodgrass, Nigel 138

Society for Animal Welfare in Israel 19, 163

Society for the Protection of Animals in North Africa 19, Notes, Ch.II.

Society for the Protection of Animals Liable to Vivisection (Victoria St. Society) 17, 27

Society for the Protection of Birds 18

Society of United Prayer for Animals (Society for United Prayer for the Prevention of Cruelty to Animals Especially with Regard to the Practice of Vivisection) 17, 100

Society of Friends in Scotland 66

Sparrow, Charles, Q.C. Notes, Ch.V, Note 1

Spooner, Glenda 41, 57

St. Andrew Animal Fund xvii, 37, 38, 40, 46, 55, 66, 157, 160, 163, Notes, Ch.XI, Note 3

Stag and deer hunting 122, 125, 184

Summerskill, Dr. Shirley, M.P. 73, 114

Tailwaggers Club Trust 163

Tealby, Mrs. 16

Textured vegetable protein 166

Thatcher, the Rt. Hon. Margaret, M.P. 100, 124

Tosh, Neil 42

Transport of animals (for slaughter) 122, 124, 158, 170, 177, 178

Traps, leg-hold (gin) 5, 6, 25, 32, 33, 79

Turkeys 131

Ulster Society for the Prevention of Cruelty to Animals 15, 163

UNESCO 84

Universal Declaration of the Rights of Animals 84, 85, 155, 169-171

Universities Federation for Animal Welfare 18, 40, 93, 148, Ch.V, Note 2

University of London Animal Welfare Society see Universities Federation for Animal Welfare

University Teach-In on Whales and Whaling, Edinburgh 79

Veal calves—intensive system 4, 5, 166, 180

Victoria St. Society—see Society for the Protection of Animals Liable to Vivisection

Vincent Wildlife Trust 86

Violence involving animals 171

Vivisection (experiments on live animals) 8, 27, 28, 29, 110, 111, 118, 119, 122, 124, 126, 132, 134, 135, 136, 142, 144, 145, 167, 170, 174, 182, 183

Vyvyan, John 18, Ch.II, Note 6

200

Walder, Angela 62
Walker, Peter, M.P. 131
Watkinson, John, M.P. 113
Webster, Canon 68
Welfare of Animals Committee (National Council of Women) 163
Westacott Ch. II, Ch.IV, Note 6
Whales xviii, xix, 79, 112, 123
White, Dr. R. J. 9
Whitehead, Phillip, M.P. 69, 114
Whiting, David 41, 56
Whitley Animal Protection Trust 46, 163
Whittaker, Alan 57, 118
Wilberforce, William 15

Wild birds 112
Williamson, Mrs. 18
Wood Green Animal Shelter 20, 163
Worcester Animal Protection Association 163
Wordsworth, William 14
World Day of Prayer for Animals 17, 68
World Federation for the Protection of Animals (British Committee) 163
World League Against Vivisection 17
World Wildlife Fund 47

Zoos and wildlife parks 11, 114, 125, 175